TRADE AND MARITIME TRANSPORT TRENDS IN THE PACIFIC

NOVEMBER 2020

ASIAN DEVELOPMENT BANK

 Creative Commons Attribution 3.0 IGO license (CC BY 3.0 IGO)

© 2020 Asian Development Bank
6 ADB Avenue, Mandaluyong City, 1550 Metro Manila, Philippines
Tel +63 2 8632 4444; Fax +63 2 8636 2444
www.adb.org

Some rights reserved. Published in 2020.

ISBN 978-92-9262-430-9 (print); 978-92-9262-431-6 (electronic); 978-92-9262-432-3 (ebook)
Publication Stock No. TCS200294-2
DOI: http://dx.doi.org/10.22617/TCS200294-2

The views expressed in this publication are those of the authors and do not necessarily reflect the views and policies of the Asian Development Bank (ADB) or its Board of Governors or the governments they represent.

ADB does not guarantee the accuracy of the data included in this publication and accepts no responsibility for any consequence of their use. The mention of specific companies or products of manufacturers does not imply that they are endorsed or recommended by ADB in preference to others of a similar nature that are not mentioned.

By making any designation of or reference to a particular territory or geographic area, or by using the term "country" in this document, ADB does not intend to make any judgments as to the legal or other status of any territory or area.

This work is available under the Creative Commons Attribution 3.0 IGO license (CC BY 3.0 IGO) https://creativecommons.org/licenses/by/3.0/igo/. By using the content of this publication, you agree to be bound by the terms of this license. For attribution, translations, adaptations, and permissions, please read the provisions and terms of use at https://www.adb.org/terms-use#openaccess.

This CC license does not apply to non-ADB copyright materials in this publication. If the material is attributed to another source, please contact the copyright owner or publisher of that source for permission to reproduce it. ADB cannot be held liable for any claims that arise as a result of your use of the material.

Please contact pubsmarketing@adb.org if you have questions or comments with respect to content, or if you wish to obtain copyright permission for your intended use that does not fall within these terms, or for permission to use the ADB logo.

Corrigenda to ADB publications may be found at http://www.adb.org/publications/corrigenda.

Note:
In this publication, "$" refers to United States dollars.

Cover design by Edith Creus.

On the cover: The Interisland Shipping Support Project will finance a new interisland shipping terminal in Vanuatu's capital, Port Vila, with improved berthing facilities, along with new and upgraded jetties on five outer islands (left); Apia Harbour in Samoa (right). Photos by ADB.

www.ingramcontent.com/pod-product-compliance
Lightning Source LLC
Chambersburg PA
CBHW060941170426
43195CB00026B/3001

Contents

Figures and Boxes iv

Foreword v

Acknowledgments vi

Abbreviations vii

Executive Summary viii
    Overview of Trade Forecasts in the Pacific Region viii
    Freight Shipping Networks and Trade Volume Forecasts at Pacific Seaports ix
    Common Trends, Challenges, and Needs across the Pacific Seaports ix

1 Overview of Trade Forecasts in the Pacific Region 1
    1.1   Overview 1
    1.2   Imports and Exports Value Profile 1
    1.3   Future Imports and Exports Value 3
    1.4   Current Trade Patterns 4
    1.5   Implications on Freight and Logistics Networks 6

2 Seaports—Freight Shipping Networks and Trade Volume Forecast 7
    2.1   International Freight Shipping Networks in the Pacific 7
    2.2   Gateway Trade Volume Forecasts 9

3 Seaports—Common Trends, Challenges, and Needs 12
    3.1   Introduction 12
    3.2   Geography and Trade Structure 12
    3.3   Import Substitution and Renewable Energy 13
    3.4   Tourism—the "Invisible Export" 15
    3.5   Cruise Liner and Port Operations 16
    3.6   Consumer Needs and Freight Shipping Patterns 17
    3.7   Regional Cooperation and Integration 18
    3.8   Climate Change Risks 20
    3.9   Exposure to Natural Hazards Risks 21
    3.10 Common Development Issues 22

4 Recent Asian Development Bank Approaches in Project Development 28
    4.1   Recent Challenges in Pacific Ports 30

Appendix: Gateway Seaports Trade Outlook 36

References 40

Figures and Boxes

Figures

1.1	Import Value Forecasts, 2015	2
1.2	Export Value Forecasts, 2015	3
1.3	Intra–Pacific Developing Member Countries Trade, 2015	4
1.4	Imports to Six Pacific Developing Member Countries, 2015	5
1.5	Exports from Six Pacific Developing Member Countries, 2015	5
2.1	Regional Shipping Capacity	8
2.2	Forecast Total TEU Throughput Growth at Six Pacific Developing Member Countries Seaports, 2015–2035	10
3.1	Typical Transition of a Multipurpose Port in the Pacific	23
4.1	Asian Development Bank Strategy 2030	28

Boxes

1	Challenges of Demand Forecasting in the Pacific	11
2	Renewable Energy in the Pacific	14
3	Solar Energy Potential in the Pacific—Solomon Islands	15
4	Tourism in the Pacific	16
5	Operational Priorities	29

Foreword

The Pacific developing member countries (DMCs) of the Asian Development Bank (ADB) rely heavily on imports to meet demand for basic goods. Key imports move primarily by maritime transport and include food, fuel, medicine, and productive resources like commercial machinery and appliances. Conversely, the export baskets of the Pacific DMCs are typically small in value and consist of a limited range of goods—often resulting in negative trade balances.

Improving trade facilitation, by upgrading seaport infrastructure and trade practices, can reduce the cost of goods and services, and improve the quality of life for communities across the Pacific. Accordingly, ADB is implementing a pipeline of projects and technical assistance to help the Pacific DMCs improve transport connectivity and overcome barriers to efficient trade. Understanding trade profiles and obstacles to efficiency is an essential first step for designing effective support to address barriers to trade.

This study seeks to fill knowledge gaps surrounding maritime trade in the region. It reviews current and projected trade patterns in the Pacific DMCs, and subsequently, provides a needs assessment and select recommendations on how to address constraints. The study represents a unique approach to supporting trade facilitation—it looks at shared constraints affecting the Pacific DMCs, such as climate change and exposure to external shocks, and seeks to identify synergistic and regional approaches to address them.

The contents of this report are made all the more relevant in the context of the coronavirus pandemic. Developing efficient infrastructure and trade practices is of central importance to reducing the costs of trade, and in turn, enabling governments to use limited financial and technical resources where they are needed most. Although this study was commissioned prior to the pandemic—and its projections do not factor in potential impacts of the virus on trade—recommendations on how to ease negative trade balances and build resilience to external shocks will be of premier importance to economic recovery and sustained growth amid global economic uncertainty. ADB will continue to work closely with its Pacific DMCs to monitor the impacts of the pandemic on trade flows, and to deliver responsive support as appropriate.

Leah Gutierrez
Director General
Pacific Department

Acknowledgments

This publication was commissioned by the Asian Development Bank, under the regional technical assistance for *Trade and Transport Facilitation in the Pacific* (RETA 8674). The Government of Japan financed the technical assistance on a grant basis, through the Japan Fund for Poverty Reduction. The Asian Development Bank wishes to acknowledge the valuable inputs and contributions of all stakeholders that contributed to this piece.

Robert Andrew Cochrane (Team Leader, ICF), Gabriella A. Bazzano (Project Director, ICF), and Shun Iwazaki (Economist, ICF) prepared the publication, with inputs and under the overall guidance of Alexandra Pamela Chiang (Senior Transport Specialist, Transport Sector Group, Sustainable Development and Climate Change Department) and Cha-Sang Shim (Transport Specialist, Pacific Department). Dong Kyu Lee (Director, Transport Division, Pacific Department) provided support and direction while preparing the publication, and Mary France Rull Creus (Associate Project Analyst) provided technical assistance administration support. Cecilia Caparas and Raymond De Vera (Knowledge Management Officers) managed the production process.

Abbreviations

ADB	–	Asian Development Bank
DMC	–	developing member country
DWT	–	tons deadweight
EEZ	–	exclusive economic zone
ENSO	–	El Niño–Southern Oscillation
ft	–	feet
LNG	–	liquefied natural gas
MHC	–	mobile harbor cranes
PRC	–	People's Republic of China
RETA	–	regional technical assistance
SDG	–	Sustainable Development Goal
SIPA	–	Solomon Islands Ports Authority
TEU	–	twenty-foot equivalent unit

Executive Summary

This study examines trade flows in six of the Pacific developing member countries (DMCs) of the Asian Development Bank (ADB): Fiji, Papua New Guinea, Samoa, Timor-Leste, Tonga, and Vanuatu.[a] It seeks to inform long-term planning to support trade facilitation initiatives across the region. It does so by raising key questions for governments and development partners to consider when designing trade and transport initiatives in the Pacific DMCs. The study addresses core questions including how trade flows in the region are changing, how growth will impact seaport operations and shipping services, and what measures can be taken to improve trade efficiency in the evolving context of trade in the Pacific.

Chapter 1 provides an overview of current and projected import and exports, trade patterns, and logistics networks. Chapter 2 examines the extent to which international freight shipping networks serve the Pacific DMCs—considering current and projected demand for shipping. Chapter 3 discusses trends across seaports in the six countries, highlighting potential interventions to improve trade balances and resilience to external shocks; and Chapter 4 provides case studies of ADB-financed initiatives that are addressing trade bottlenecks in the region. Highlights from the report are elaborated on below.

Trade Forecasts for the Region

Petroleum products (namely fuel) comprise the largest share of imports by value into the six Pacific DMCs. Other key imports include industrial and commercial machinery, appliances, and food. In line with population and economic growth, imports across the six Pacific DMCs are projected to grow by 40%–50% from 2015 to 2035. Papua New Guinea, Timor-Leste, and (to a lesser extent) Fiji will account for the majority of this expansion, corresponding to forecasts for population and economic growth in each nation, respectively.

Projections for exports in the six nations (by value) are more varied than for import. At present, exports from the smaller economies (Samoa, Tonga, and Vanuatu) consist largely of animal and vegetable products, while exports from Fiji and Papua New Guinea are more diverse. Papua New Guinea is the largest exporter of the six economies, due to mineral exports including liquified natural gas; while Fiji has a relatively developed tourism sector. The impacts of growing export volumes on trade logistics (and potentially, demand for freight shipping) will be most pronounced in Papua New Guinea, as it has the largest potential to increase its export market.

Trade partnerships across the Pacific are expanding. Imports into the six Pacific DMCs originate from a range of trade partners in the Pacific Ocean (including Australia, New Zealand, Singapore, and the Untied States). Papua New Guinea dominates exports from the Pacific, with products destined to a range of international trading partners, including Australia and Japan. Intra-Pacific DMCs trade is very low, primarily due to the uniformity of potential

---

[a] The study was commissioned in 2016 and completed in 2020. At the time of inception, Timor-Leste was classified as a Pacific DMCs, but has since been reclassified as a Southeast Asian DMC.

exports produced in each of the six nations. Looking ahead, the larger Asian economies are expected to take on an increasing role as trade partners with the Pacific DMCs, in addition to ongoing trade with conventional partners like Australia and New Zealand.

Freight Shipping Networks and Trade Volume Forecasts at Pacific Seaports

Seaports in the Pacific DMCs are served primarily by small, mixed cargo and container vessels, with typical capacity of up to 900 twenty-foot equivalent units (TEUs). These ships link the Pacific DMCs to main trading partners via regional hub ports (including through Suva Port in Fiji and Lae Port in Papua New Guinea), forming an arc of freight services concentrated around the Western Pacific down to Australia and New Zealand.

The frequency of international container services has improved over time and currently provides adequate service levels to meet import and export demands in the Pacific DMCs. As such, a focus area for shipping lines going forward will be to improve the efficiency and cost-effectiveness of their services by increasing vessel size, rather than increasing the frequency of services. Accordingly, the size of container vessels is expected to gradually increase to 2,500–3,000 TEUs, which is deemed adequate to accommodate projected traffic demand in the region.

The study presents a detailed analysis on gateway seaports in Fiji, Papua New Guinea, Samoa, Timor-Leste, Tonga, and Vanuatu. Given that import volumes are often dominant at the six ports, import traffic (as opposed to exports) typically determines trade flows. Accordingly, growth in total container throughput volumes during 2015–2035 is expected to double in Papua New Guinea and Timor-Leste (which possess relatively higher underlying economic and population growth potentials) and to increase by approximately 40%–60% in the other four countries, which have more gradual economic and population growth projections.

Common Trends, Challenges, and Needs across the Pacific Seaports

The Pacific DMCs share common characteristics that affect their trade profiles, port sizes, and port operations. The study looks at eight themes that affect ports in the region, and concludes with a review of shared development issues. The eight topics are: (i) geography and trade structures, (ii) import substitution potential, (iii) tourism, (iv) cruise liners, (v) consumer needs, (vi) regional cooperation and integration, (vii) climate risks, and (viii) exposure to natural hazards. Due to endemic factors that limit exports—such as few natural resources, and small economies of scale that restrict export sectors like manufacturing—trade flows in the Pacific will continue to be governed by laden import container (which determine required port facilities), while exports will be dominated by back-loaded empty containers.

This structure results in negative balance of payments, and exposes the Pacific economies to external shocks. Import substitution—the practice of reducing import demand by leveraging domestic resources—can play a key role in addressing negative balance of payments and reducing vulnerability to external shocks. Noting the heavy weight of fuel (for power generation) in Pacific import portfolios, the study highlights the role that increased renewable energy generation can play in lowering fuel imports and helping level off negative trade balances.

The study also highlights that ports in the Pacific are multipurposed—catering to container vessels, fishing vessels, and cruise liners simultaneously—and in cases, are outdated. Trade expansion, containerization, and the increased frequency and severity of exposure to natural hazards are progressively changing requirements for infrastructure and operations. Some of the emerging themes that will require further support from the development community include the need to upgrade port infrastructure to protect against exposure to natural hazards and climate change, and the growing importance of terminal separation—evidenced, in part, by traffic disruptions caused by cruise liners taking priority over other port traffic.

The study concludes with a review of short- and long-term opportunities for development partners and Pacific DMC governments to consider as they continue to facilitate and expand on regional trade flows. There is no "one-size-fits-all" solution to port development in the region. However, the study proposes a phased approach to ongoing development, taking into account resource constraints alongside projected growth in port demand. The phased approach seeks to balance progressive infrastructure upgrades with soft interventions to support the Pacific DMCs in providing adequate capacity while optimizing efficiency.

1 Overview of Trade Forecasts in the Pacific Region

1.1 Overview

This chapter presents the baseline trade volume and freight flows for the Pacific developing member countries (DMCs) that participated in the study. These are Fiji, Papua New Guinea, Samoa, Timor-Leste (footnote a), Tonga, and Vanuatu (hereinafter referred to as the six Pacific DMCs). At the time of the study, the base year was defined as 2015. The import and export values of each country for the base year and forecast years of 2025 and 2035 were produced.

1.2 Imports and Exports Value Profile

The most striking aspect of their imports value profile, which is common across the six Pacific DMCs, is that a large proportion goes to mineral products, which mainly consist of refined petroleum products ranging from heavy fuel oils used for electricity generation to distilled diesel and petrol (gasoline) fuels, and the contribution of other minerals (such as ores and cement clinker) in value terms is negligible. Industrial and commercial machinery, mechanical appliances, and vehicles also comprise a big proportion of the imports value profile. This can be affected in value terms by items such as imported passenger aircraft, imported seagoing vessels, and heavy machinery and construction equipment for large infrastructure projects. The dominance of these import items are likely to be overlooked when assessing container volumes as they are mostly imported as bulk liquids (petroleum) and break bulk (machinery and vehicles), although machinery and vehicles are now transported in containers more frequently. Commodity groups 1–3[1] together comprise the total imports value of food, which generally account for around 20%–30% of imports (Figure 1.1).

The exports value profile of the six Pacific DMCs is much more varied than that of imports, although the smaller countries tend to have limited export opportunities. Most of the smaller countries' exports consist of animal and vegetable products. These cover fish, vegetables, copra, coffee, and coconut oil which are the primary merchandise exports for Samoa, Tonga, and Vanuatu. Timor-Leste exports are primarily coffee beans with a small amount of other agricultural products. Fiji has one of the most diversified export systems of all, with a broad range of exports including agricultural produce, mineral water, chemicals, textiles, cement, and timber products. Papua New Guinea has the largest export base, with $9.3 billion in exports value in 2015. This is primarily natural resources, with significant exports of petroleum products, mineral/metal resources such as gold and copper, and timber as well as agricultural exports such as coffee. Papua New Guinea's exports have grown significantly in recent years, led by the mineral products category following the opening of an Exxon-Mobil liquefied natural gas (LNG) facility in 2014 (Figure 1.2).

---

[1] This includes: live animals, animal products (including fish) (commodity group 1, equivalent to HS [refer to definition of Pacific Rim countries and trading partners in footnote 2 and alternative scenarios for future possible outcomes in footnote 3] Section 1); vegetable products (commodity group 2, equivalent to HS Section 2); and fats and oil, prepared foodstuff, beverages (commodity group 3, equivalent to HS Sections 3 and 4)

Figure 1.1: Import Value Forecasts, 2015
($ million)

Note:

1. The analyses were conducted based on the international Harmonized System (HS) commodities classification.
2. The international Harmonised System is an international system of names and numbers used to describe trade, developed by the World Customs Organization.

Source: Asian Development Bank (Pacific Department).

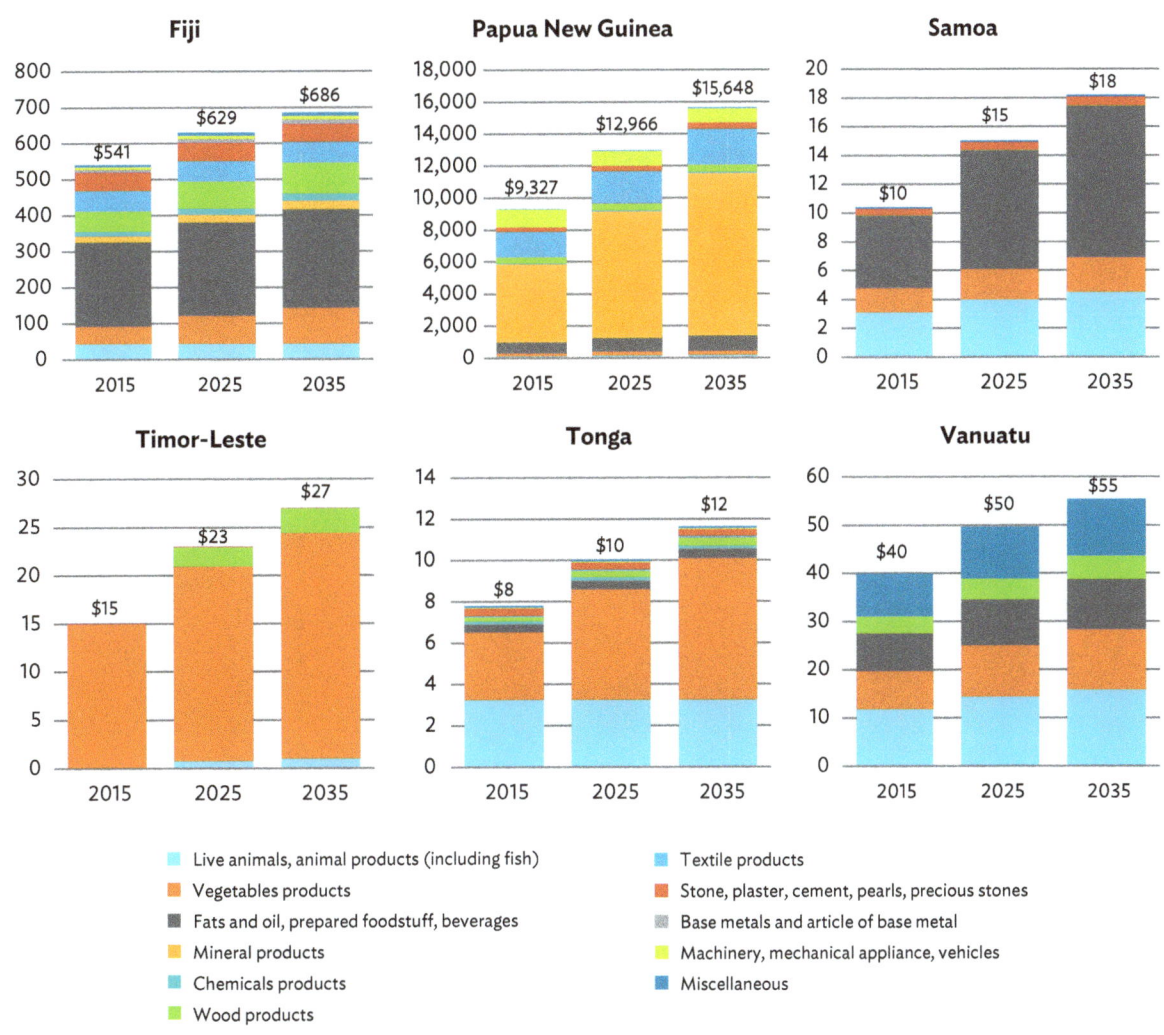

Figure 1.2: Export Value Forecasts, 2015
($ million)

Note:
1. The analyses were conducted based on the international Harmonized System (HS) commodities classification.
2. The international Harmonized System is an international system of names and numbers used to describe trade, developed by the World Customs Organization.

Source: Asian Development Bank (Pacific Department).

1.3 Future Imports and Exports Value

The future growth in imports is forecast to be the highest for countries with both high population and high economic growth rates. This includes Timor-Leste and Papua New Guinea and to a lesser extent, Fiji. Countries with lower rates of population and economic growth such as Samoa and Tonga are forecast to have modest growth in imports over the forecast period. The total growth in imports over the 20-year forecasts period is around 40%–50% for most of the six Pacific DMCs.

The scale of export growth differs significantly across the six Pacific DMCs, and although countries such as Timor-Leste may experience strong growth in percentage terms, the magnitude of increases is only in the tens of millions of dollars. For a country of over 1 million people, the impact of these changes is relatively minor. Papua New Guinea, by contrast, is already by far the largest exporter of all and has many export expansion possibilities. The most significant of these is likely to be further expansion of its LNG reserves, the timing of which will depend on the recovery of resource prices.

1.4 Current Trade Patterns

Figure 1.3 shows the pattern of trade between the Pacific DMCs. With the exception of trade with the two largest countries (Papua New Guinea and Fiji), the level of intraregional trade is very low. This is attributed to the small populations of the island archipelago countries and the uniformity of their potential exports reducing the scope for trade.

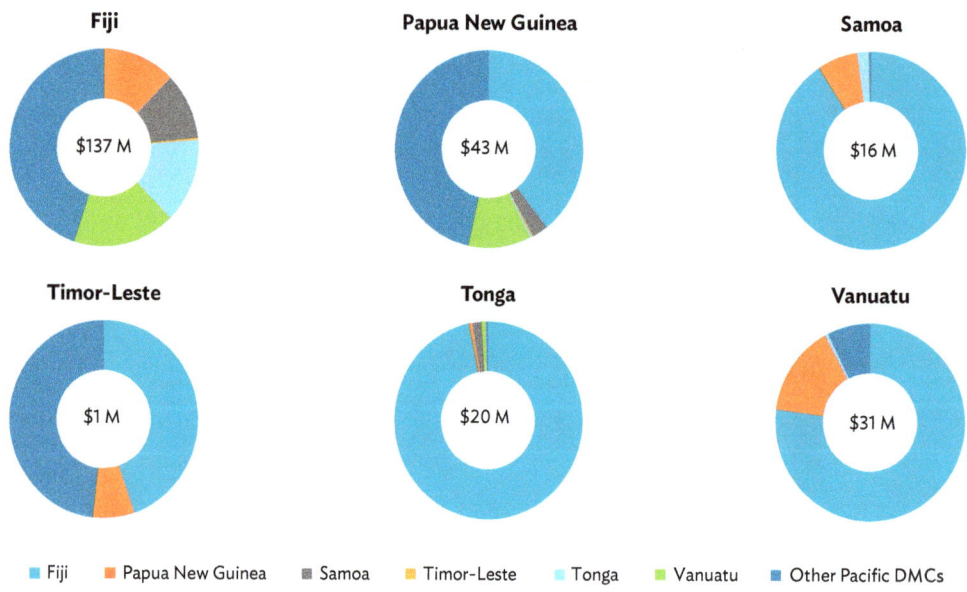

Figure 1.3: Intra–Pacific Developing Member Countries' Trade, 2015

DMC = developing member country.
Note: Imports and exports between country pairs have been aggregated (trade value = imports to country A from country B + exports from country A to country B).
Source: Asian Development Bank (Pacific Department).

Imports to the six Pacific DMCs (Figure 1.4) are evenly spread across the major trading partners among the Pacific Rim countries, with Singapore having a large share due to its petroleum exports.[2] Exports from the six Pacific DMCs (Figure 1.5) are dominated by outputs from Papua New Guinea, which are spread across a number of trading partners.

---

[2] For the purpose of this study, Pacific Rim countries mean the countries that lie along the Pacific Ocean. They include some of the biggest trading partners of the six Pacific DMCs, such as Australia, Japan, New Zealand, the People's Republic of China, Singapore, and the United States.

Overview of Trade Forecasts in the Pacific Region

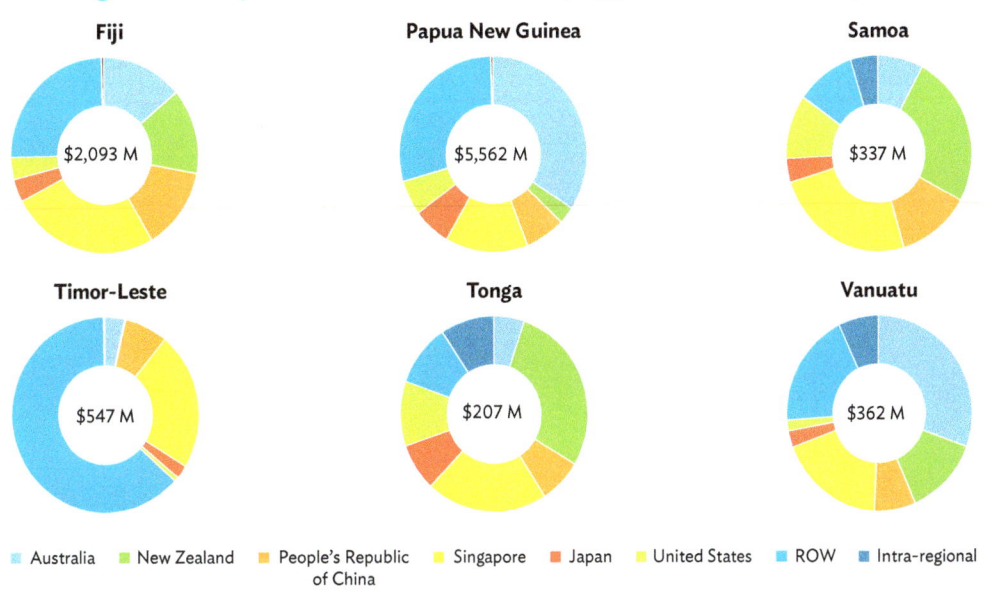

Figure 1.4: Imports to Six Pacific Developing Member Countries, 2015

ROW = rest of the world.
Note: The figures depict origin of imports to each Pacific developing member country in 2015, while the total value of the trade is shown in the center and is in United States dollars.
Source: Asian Development Bank (Pacific Department).

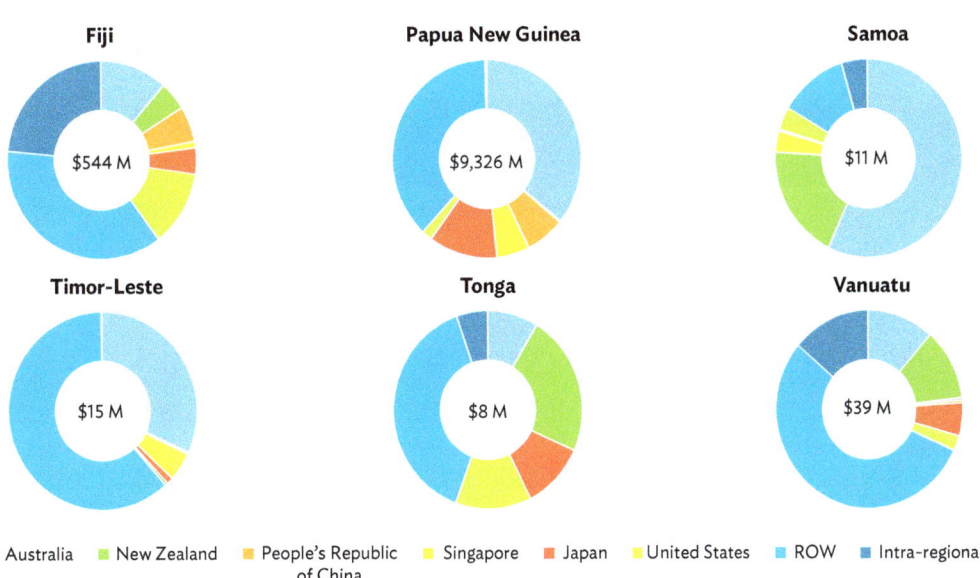

Figure 1.5: Exports from Six Pacific Developing Member Countries, 2015

ROW = rest of the world.
Note: The figures depict destination of exports from each Pacific developing member country in 2015, while the total value of the trade is shown in the center and is in United States dollars.
Source: Asian Development Bank (Pacific Department).

1.5 Implications for Freight and Logistics Networks

In terms of regional trade, there are no current indications that regional trade flows will significantly change.

While the overall import volumes will increase in absolute terms driven primarily by population and economic growth of each Pacific DMC, it is projected that their profile will largely remain the same and major trading partners among the Pacific Rim countries will continue to be the most important source of imports to the Pacific DMCs.

Most of the smaller Pacific DMCs will continue to produce a relatively homogenous collection of agricultural and fisheries products that will be exported outside the region. There will be continued opportunities for the regional hubs of Fiji and Papua New Guinea to move up the value chain by undertaking processing activities to supply the smaller island nations. However, for the most part the Pacific DMCs will continue to position their primary industries as high-quality export produce aimed at the traditional trading partners in Australia, New Zealand, and the United States, and increasingly the growing middle class in Southeast Asia and East Asia.

This means that while the sea and air networks in the region will need to expand their capacities, the changes in the patterns of trade are unlikely by themselves to drive significant changes in the networks.

2 Seaports—Freight Shipping Networks and Trade Volume Forecast

2.1 International Freight Shipping Networks in the Pacific

This study focuses mainly on the international freight shipping network in the Pacific. The current capacity and potential future developments to meet the forecast seaborne freight demand have been assessed.

Other than for crude oil and ores exports primarily from Papua New Guinea, the bulk shipping demand comprises mostly refined petroleum imports, supplied almost entirely from refineries in Singapore. Products are distributed by tankers in vessel capacity ranging from 20,000–30,000 tons deadweight (DWT) (Handysized) both directly to individual Pacific DMCs and via the import and transshipment terminal in Suva, Fiji, using seagoing powered barges for onward distribution. Niue is an exception, where fuel that originates from Singapore is supplied from New Zealand in tanktainers.

Global distribution of non-bulk freight by sea is now handled almost entirely by large specialized vessels. New cars and other transport vehicles are carried in large ro-ro (roll-on/roll-off) vessels and, with the exception of large construction components and large fabricated items (for example, quay cranes for large container terminals and offshore oil and gas facility components), freight is wherever possible unitized. Cars (both new and previously used) are delivered from Pacific Rim countries to smaller Pacific DMCs either by mixed ro-ro and container vessels or in containers.

The major intercontinental flows are carried by a small number of large shipping lines and consortia, operating vessels up to 20,000 TEUs in capacity, up to 400 meters in length overall and over 200,000 DWT. These shipping lines carry high volumes of goods across the Pacific between the Pacific Rim countries in vessels of up to about 13,000 TEUs capacity, either directly or via transshipment ports such as Busan (Republic of Korea), Singapore, and Tauranga (New Zealand). In the past, these lines also operated smaller vessels serving the Pacific DMCs (for example, Maersk operated a shuttle service between New Zealand and Fiji), but now only two major lines, CMA CGM and Hamburg Sud, operate long-distance trans-Pacific services calling at ports within the Pacific, although Maersk and Matson operate specific services with smaller vessels from the Malacca Straits and New Zealand, respectively.

The Pacific DMCs themselves are served by smaller regional vessels linking them to the Pacific Rim countries and hub ports. These services are provided by a relatively large number of smaller shipping lines, operating individually or as members of consortia. Two main types of service may be distinguished: shuttle services for major links to the larger countries (such as those from New Zealand to Fiji) and longer "string" services connected particular groups of Pacific Rim countries to groups of Pacific DMCs.

An example of the former is the Neptune shuttle which links Auckland and Tauranga in New Zealand with Lautoka and Suva in Fiji. This also illustrates another characteristic—services may make two calls in a single country, since the main "gateway" port for imports is often located in the capital, whereas the majority of agricultural exports may be exported from a second and slightly smaller port at which export flows exceed imports.

Examples of the second type of service are the Swire Shipping services in the Western Pacific, the Kyowa Line and Bali Hai Consortium services linking the North East Asian countries with the Pacific DMCs in the West and South Pacific, and the newly introduced AUSPAC and SOUTHPAC Consortia services linking Australia and New Zealand, respectively, with the Pacific DMCs in the South Pacific.

Two types of vessels currently provide these regional services. The first is a mixed-cargo vessel, generally of about 18,000 DWT providing ro-ro decks for new cars together with a mix of general cargo holds and container frames. The second is a small container vessel, typically of about 13,000 DWT and carrying up to 900 TEUs. These vessels carry all the necessary handling equipment for loading and unloading, including both ship's gear such as cranes or derricks, and where appropriate, ro-ro ramps. The majority of imports are carried in standard 20 feet (ft) containers which are re-exported empty. Exports include perishable food and agricultural products such as frozen fish and squash carried in 40 ft reefer containers, which are re-imported empty.

Approximately 80% of containers are currently 20 ft, much higher than the global figure of about 50%, with only 20% being 40 ft in 2016. The reason is the dominance of imports to relatively small populations and the need for regular supplies in smaller quantities. This is now changing in the larger countries with populations of 300,000 or more with a steady move to 40 ft containers to reduce unit costs.

The total service capacity provided between the Pacific Rim countries and the Pacific DMCs is shown in Figure 2.1. The concentration of capacity forms an arc round the Western Pacific Rim countries down to Australia and out into New Zealand. The capacity of the Pacific DMCs in the North Pacific is much lower, reflecting the small populations and trade levels of these widely spread archipelagos.

Figure 2.1: Regional Shipping Capacity

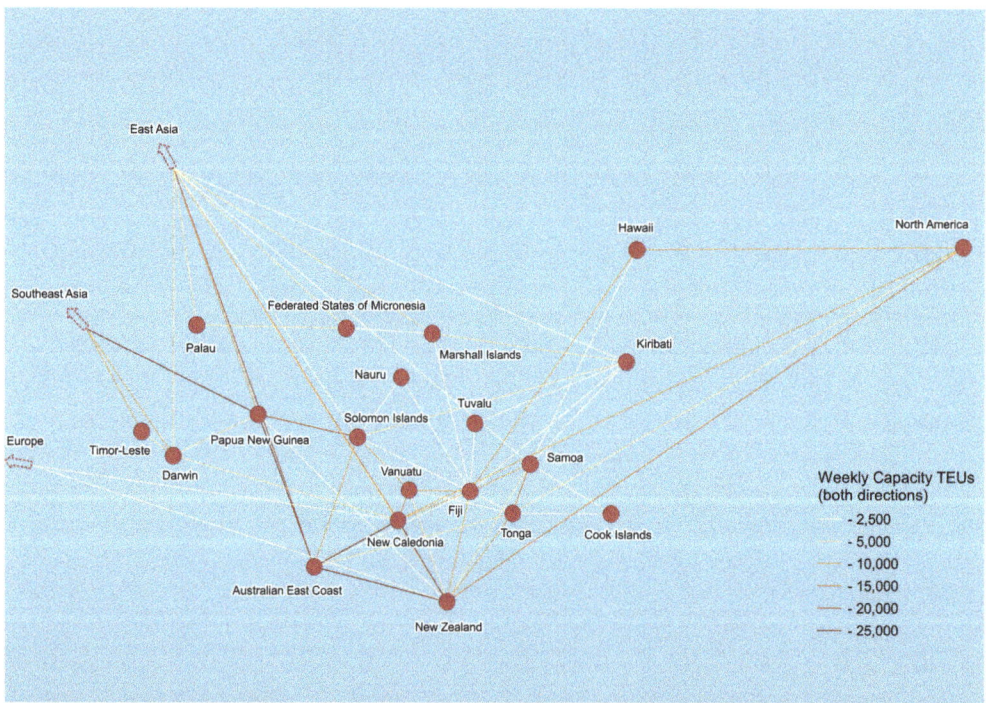

TEU = twenty-foot equivalent unit.
Note: East Asia includes Japan, the Republic of Korea, China, Hong Kong and Taipei,China; North America includes Canada and US; South East Asia includes Singapore, Malaysia and Indonesia
Source: Asian Development Bank (Pacific Department).

Interviews with freight forwarders have confirmed that the current freight network capacity is adequate to serve the Pacific. However, the frequencies of services have been too low and poorly scheduled in the past. This changed at the time when this study commenced in 2016–2017 as consortia developed joint services providing scheduled services approximately every 2 weeks between all the major international "gateway" ports and the Pacific Rim countries and weekly for the shorter shuttle services on high-density links such as the New Zealand–Fiji service. Of the countries studied in detail, only Tuvalu and Niue now have lower service frequencies, due to their small size and geographical isolation.

An attempt has been made to forecast the future changes in the pattern of shipping serving the Pacific DMCs as a result of the forecast growth in trade. This includes the likely size and nature of the vessels used in the future, which will influence the needed port improvements. Based on discussions with shipping lines, comparisons with shipping networks elsewhere, and taking into account the economies of scale associated with the use of larger vessels, the following conclusions have been drawn:

- Now that the frequencies of international container services have improved to every 2 weeks (from as infrequently as once monthly) for all the main routes and weekly on those with the highest flows, shipping lines will concentrate on improving the efficiency and cost-effectiveness of services by increasing vessel sizes to take advantage of the economies of scale associated with larger vessels, rather than further improving frequencies.
- Since even with the highest levels of growth forecast, container flows will still in general be less than double the existing flows, container vessel sizes will still for the most part be less than 2,500–3,000 TEUs. This forecast has been confirmed by Swire and Maersk.
- Most of the ports will still have throughputs, which do not justify providing expensive and difficult to maintain quay cranes, so the ships will continue to provide their own ships' gear cranes, supplemented by mobile harbor cranes (MHCs) at the larger ports loading and unloading higher numbers of containers per vessel.
- The larger ports, such as Suva Port, may have the potential to become transshipment hubs in the longer term. That is a matter for further assessment in the separate detailed study. However, there is unlikely to be yard capacity for transshipment in Suva without the development of a new container terminal location. If consortium services such as AUSPAC and SOUTHPAC can provide adequate levels of capacity and service without the additional costs of transshipment, the present shipping network appears likely to remain without significant change for the next decade.

2.2 Gateway Trade Volume Forecasts

More detailed analyses were conducted for gateway seaports in Fiji, Papua New Guinea, Samoa, Timor-Leste, Tonga, and Vanuatu. Figure 2.2 summarizes the forecast total TEU throughput growth rates by volume for the six Pacific DMCs gateway seaports under different growth scenarios. In addition to the base case projections, which is the central estimate of total TEU throughput by gateway seaport in 2035, a scenario approach[3] was used to reflect possible future outcomes. In doing so, a range of possible forecast values is identified, the upper and lower bounds of which can then be interpreted as the relative optimistic and pessimistic scenarios for TEU throughput at each gateway seaport.

---

[3] The first alternative scenario is based on an analysis of TEU throughput per capita and its relationship to per capita gross domestic product (GDP) in individual countries. The second alternative scenario assumes that lower productivity growth in the six Pacific DMCs will hinder their economic advancement and the growing balance of trade deficits will constrain both export and import growth.

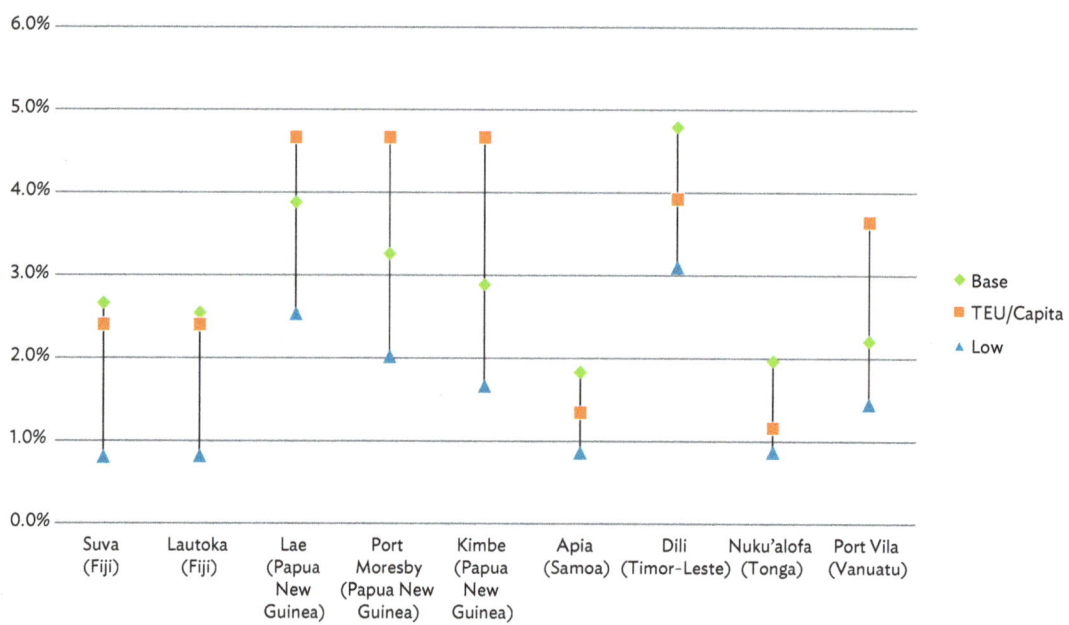

Figure 2.2: Forecast Total TEU Throughput Growth at Six Pacific Developing Member Countries' Seaports, 2015–2035

TEU = twenty-foot equivalent unit.
Source: Asian Development Bank (Pacific Department).

The key factors raised by these gateway seaport volume forecasts include:

- The most important bulk cargo for all these ports is refined petroleum products to produce baseload power for land, sea, and air transport. This is imported almost entirely from Singapore since the Australian and New Zealand refining capacities are now negligible. Imports are either directly by tankers serving a string of country and island terminals or via the oil hub at Suva, Fiji, with onward delivery by small tankers or seagoing oil barges. All Pacific DMCs are attempting to reduce their dependency on petroleum product imports using alternative energy sources. The degree to which this will be successful depends on the respective countries. For example, Fiji increasingly obtains much of the baseload electricity on the larger islands from hydropower, and energy imports will be directed primarily to transport. Smaller archipelago countries are also seeking to substitute residual fuel oil and diesel fuels used for baseload generation by means of solar and wind energy. It is worth noting that trade with Singapore also affects exports from the Pacific DMCs—Papua New Guinea exports crude oil to Singapore and imports refined products.
- Import container volumes are dominant at the majority of Pacific DMCs ports, thus the growth in imports will determine capacity constraints, other than at specific smaller export-oriented ports such as Lautoka (near Nadi, Fiji).
- Some countries have recently had large construction projects relative to the size of their economies as a result of both national infrastructure development projects and reconstruction after exposure to natural hazards, primarily tropical cyclones including Cyclone Winston in Fiji and Cyclone Pam in Vanuatu. These affect imports in two ways. First, directly through imported materials for the project and second, indirectly as job growth and spending in the economy increase local incomes and this leads to greater consumption of imports.
- Faster container export growth, while good for the economy, will not impact on port volumes materially as they are mostly back-loading of empty containers. The exception is exports of fish and small quantities of

- high-quality perishable vegetables such as Tongan squash for which 40 ft reefers are seasonally imported empty.
- Several ports have experienced fast growth in import container volumes in the previous 5–10 years. The resulting current account deficits have been supported by international development assistance and in many cases by a high level of remittances. It is unlikely that these will continue to increase at the current rates and therefore import volumes are expected to grow more slowly.
- General cargo and road vehicles, together with bulk cargo carried in volumes, which do not justify dry bulk freighters, are increasingly being carried in containers, leading to growth in the container component of freight in recent years being faster than the underlying growth in sea freight. This switch will be completed in the coming decade, leading to a slower rate of long-term container growth driven by total trade.
- Overall growth in container throughput across the 20-year forecast period is expected to be around 100% (about 3.5% per annum) for countries with growing economies and high underlying population growth (Papua New Guinea and Timor-Leste). For the countries with slower economic growth and stagnant populations, total container throughput is forecast to be 40%–60% higher by 2035.

Further information on the gateway seaport forecasts in the selected Pacific DMCs are included in the Appendix.

Box 1: Challenges of Demand Forecasting in the Pacific

The gateway seaport volume forecasts are based on estimates of long-term growth in the economy and hence trade growth. However, it is worth noting other factors that may contribute to additional volatility to actual growth.

One of the contributing factors is fluctuations in international aid provision. This drives additional imports of materials and equipment and also increases local employment, which in turn increases consumption of imports.

The secondary driver is the occurrence of natural hazards, which is common in the Pacific. While these risks can be mitigated, they cannot be predicted accurately. Additional aid is almost always needed for immediate relief and longer-term recovery, leading to unpredictable surges in aid and aid-related trade.

In the very short term, some of these variations from the long-term trend can be assessed from committed aid programs, but even here, the accuracy of forecasting year to year volatility is weak in countries with multiple bilateral aid programs. As such, seaborne trade in any particular year can only be forecast as lying within a band, which extends above and below the long-term trend line.

3 Seaports—Common Trends, Challenges, and Needs

3.1 Introduction

Seaports in the Pacific share common transport needs and challenges. Key themes, which impact both maritime trade and freight needs on demand side, and infrastructure needs on the supply side include:

- Geography and Trade Structure
- Import Substitution and Renewable Energy
- Tourism—the "Invisible Export"
- Cruise Liner and Port Operations
- Consumer Needs and Freight Shipping Patterns
- Regional Cooperation and Integration
- Climate Change Risks
- Exposure to Natural Hazards
- Common Development Issues

Each of them is reviewed below in this chapter.

3.2 Geography and Trade Structure

The most important underlying variation between the seaports in the Pacific is their size and the effect of scale. The population of the countries served by these seaports range from over 8 million in Papua New Guinea, down to about 1,600 in Niue.

General Characteristics Affecting Trade, Port Size, and Port Operations

In most of the smaller Pacific DMCs, a higher percentage of the population tends to live in the capital or near the capital and on the same island. The other towns and villages tend to be small, so the population often divide into an urban group, concentrated in and near the capital, and rural villages, where the population practices a subsistence agricultural economy, growing fruit and vegetables for their own consumption and selling the surplus to the capital population for cash to support imports of nonagricultural items.

The smaller the country, the less likely it is to have natural resources other than agricultural products which can be exported. Most agricultural products are common to all the countries, so trade between the Pacific DMCs is low. Specialized varieties such as Niue vanilla and Tongan squash are of high value, but the quantities are usually too low to make a major impact on the economy.

Fish is the major natural resource for most Pacific DMCs, which have large exclusive economic zones (EEZs). However, locally based fish processing industries are rare to be spotted due to the migratory nature of these fish resources, lack of physical infrastructure/skilled local labor, and fierce regional competition. In general, the fishing industry tends to contribute to national economy mainly through license fees from long-distance fishing vessels from East Asian countries operating in their EEZ, rather than direct export and further processing of these caught fish. This trend is expected to continue.

The smaller Pacific DMCs are unlikely ever to have domestic markets large enough to support significant manufacturing which increasingly depends on economies of scale. International container trade is thus usually dominated and governed by imports of manufactured goods, processed foods, and urban building materials, together with refined oil products for power generation and transport. This creates balance-of-payments difficulties, placing great emphasis on import substitution. The largest international general cargo and container port is almost always situated in or close to the capital, as the population with cash incomes tends to be concentrated in or close to the capital.

The larger Pacific DMCs are more likely to have mineral resources including oil and metallic ores for export. High volume exports tend to be shipped through specialized ports, often owned and operated by mines or in the case of oil, direct from offshore rigs, so they have little impact on the general cargo ports. In Timor-Leste, for instance, the major oil fields are offshore, and oil is exported directly from offshore rigs, without coming ashore, so the impact on their gateway ports is low. In Papua New Guinea, oil and gas from inland fields is transported to the coast by pipeline and exported from specialized processing complexes and wharves, away from the gateway ports. That said, crude oil and gas exports are important in the balance of trade of the Pacific Rim countries with such resources.

The larger Pacific DMCs will continue to import refined fuel and bulk gas directly from Singapore in medium-sized Handymax (20,000 to 30,000 DWT) tankers and the smaller countries will be served by small fuel tankers from regional distribution centers such as Suva, Fiji. These will continue to moor at swinging mooring buoy facilities, generally in or close to the capital's gateway port as the capital is the center of demand. Small isolated countries such as Niue are likely to continue to use tanktainers carried on container vessels instead.

- Trade will continue to be governed by laden import container flows, while main exports will be back-loaded empty containers.

Facilities required at the gateway port depend on the volumes of imports.

3.3 Import Substitution and Renewable Energy

The balance of trade by value and the balance of payments excluding aid are on average negative for all the countries in the Pacific. They thus remain financially vulnerable to natural hazards, oil prices, and any weakness in the economies of their trading partners. Import substitution wherever possible is therefore essential to minimize balance of payment deficits.

One of the most important import to the Pacific DMCs in terms of size and the possibility of substitution is mineral products. In the past, both power generation and transport have been dependent on imported refined fuels, which typically constituted about 20% of the value of imports in countries such as Solomon Islands.

Box 2: Renewable Energy in the Pacific

 Natural resources are abundant—wind, hydro power, solar etc.

 A successful implementation of renewable energy can be more difficult in markets where regulation, supply, and distribution of energy are monopolized.

 Regulatory frameworks need to be adopted by the governments.

 Renewable energy introduction and growth have not yet reached/started in several Pacific DMCs—especially smaller countries.

Source: Asian Development Bank (Pacific Department).

To reduce the dependency to the imported fuel products for power generation, Fiji has been generating hydropower since 1983 and several countries in the Pacific are developing micro-hydro schemes at village level where their topology permits. Wind tends in many countries to vary seasonally and wind power installations must also be strong enough to withstand cyclone wind strengths. However, the most successful alternative energy source common to the Pacific DMCs appears to be solar energy.

- Import substitution is essential to maintain financial immunity.
- The most important import in terms of size and the possibility of substitution is fuel products.

Solar energy appears to be the most successful alternative energy source.

This is particularly important in the case of ports. The efficiency of LED lighting means that the small power requirements for night-time lighting associated with navigation and yard operation can easily be met by local installations of solar panels and batteries mounted on the units themselves.

The power requirements for refrigerated containers in yards, and for recharging electrified cranes and heavy handling gear are much higher and will require carefully designed port-wide solar power installations. Where the ports are adjacent to large urban areas, it may be advantageous to integrate these with the national grid, with the port buying electricity from, and selling back into a solar and possibly also hydro based network. However, the transition must take account of the difficulties created for national power generation and distribution companies. The existing power supply networks distributing power from diesel generation plants do not at present have the control systems and resilience needed to control two-way flows of energy between small solar farms and to and from individual businesses.

In the meantime, where, as in Noro, a fishing town in Solomon Islands, the power requirements for refrigerating stored fish for export are a very large part of the total regional demand, a standalone solar power solution is likely to be needed. Some diesel fuel will still be needed in combination with batteries for solar energy standby. Although battery costs are falling, they are still high and battery production itself has a significant carbon footprint.

Box 3: Solar Energy Potential in the Pacific—Solomon Islands

Key Issues in Electricity Supply

- **Security** – Electricity mix is entirely diesel-based, which is import dependent and subject to price volatility. Imported diesel accounts for 96% of all power generation in Solomon Islands.

- **Price** – Solomon Islands has one of the highest electricity tariffs of all Pacific developing member countries. This affects the competitiveness of local business and makes electricity less affordable to many residents.

- **Climate** – Diesel power generation affects environment negatively by causing greenhouse gas emissions and local pollutants. Solomon Islands Ports Authority has the vision to transform Noro Port into a carbon-neutral port by 2030.[a]

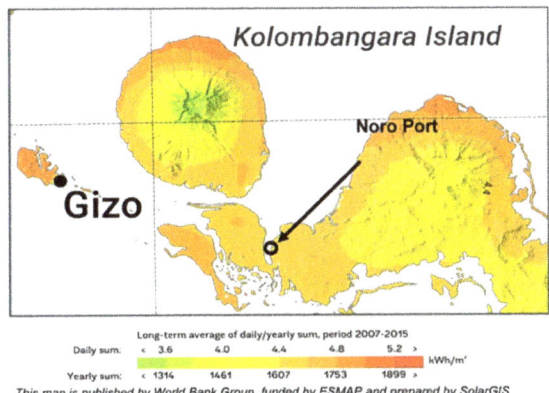

Solar Resource near Noro Port

Why Solar?

Ample sunlight – Solomon Islands has adequate solar resource, which if harvested for electricity generation, can help in local souring of electricity.

Competitive price, stable over cycle – The price of solar technology has rapidly declined thereby making solar power price competitive with conventional generation technologies. The price of solar electricity remains largely constant throughout the project cycle since the price is mainly affected by the initial capital cost.

Environment Sustainability – Solar generation does not cause greenhouse gas emission or pollutants.

[a] World Port Sustainability Program. Solomon Islands Ports Authority – Green Ports Project. https://sustainableworldports.org/project/solomon-islands-ports-authority-green-ports-project.

Source: ADB based on SolarGIS.

3.4 Tourism—the "Invisible Export"

Most of the Pacific DMCs enjoy a warm tropical climate. They are rich in culture and history, and offer beautiful sceneries to accommodate wide variety of activities for visitors.

According to the forecasts by the Pacific Asia Travel Association, an aggregate visitor number growth of about 5.5% per year is expected across the Asia and the Pacific region from 2019 to 2023. The growth in the countries in the Central Pacific which are more remote from the major origin markets is likely to be lower at about 4.4%.

Nevertheless, this represents a growth of 19% over 4 years, which would place pressure on current air services and airport passenger facilities. The quality of the air services and in particular, the ability to land efficient modern wide-bodied aircraft traveling from Pacific Rim countries and air hubs is critical. Many of the capitals in the Pacific have long runways, which are now being upgraded. In parallel, improvements in airport passenger facilities are needed, as services tend to arrive and depart at about the same time of day, so the apron areas become inadequate and terminals become overcrowded with arriving and departing passengers. Where the airports are more distant from

Box 4: Tourism in the Pacific

 Abundance of natural habitats, such as sandy beaches and a relatively consistent climate.

 Tourism is very important as a source of foreign currency—it is an "invisible export" and a source of local employment in those countries with significant unemployment.

 Smaller countries tend to have less capacity to absorb an increase in tourist numbers than the larger ones.

 It is key to build a long-term sustainable tourism sector without straining local environment and culture.

---

the capital towns and hotels, road improvements are also needed. Samoa has a program of runway, apron, and terminal improvement coupled with improvements to the coastal road linking the airport at Faleolo with Apia.

Cruise ships and recreational yachts make a considerable impact on overall visitor numbers, but not much on local accommodation needs as they are designed to provide beds and shelter to their passengers. However, given that tourism in the Pacific is largely dependent on flights, the projected increase in visitor numbers is highly correlated with those traveling by air and would require significant growth in hotel and resort accommodation as well.

From the perspective of trade forecasting and seaport development, the main issues are imports of building materials for hotel and guest house construction and imports of provisions including food and drink for visiting tourists. These require regular shipping services, with a minimum schedule of a service every 2 weeks, since tourists other than in really remote locations are unwilling to accept shortages of their daily necessities and storage for longer periods in a tropical climate is expensive.

- More tourists are projected to visit the countries in the Pacific.
- Growth in tourism will constrain airborne services and facilities, and will increase needs for tourist amenities.

> **Establishing regular shipping services is key to accommodate the projected growth in tourism.**

3.5 Cruise Liner and Port Operations

A related form of Pacific tourism is cruise liner calls. The international cruise market has expanded rapidly over the last 10 years. There were estimated to be about 220 cruise liners in service worldwide in 1998. By 2027, this figure is estimated to grow to 500–550 vessels. The size range of these vessels is varied, with small luxury and adventure cruise vessels being constructed with as few as 150 berths, midsized vessels with 1,000–2,500 berths, and large cruise liners with up to 5,500 berths.

The average cruise length worldwide is about 7 days, with most passengers expecting to visit three or four destinations and return to their home port. Many cruises from Australian ports, which are main points of departure to the countries in the Pacific, correspond to this pattern, with cruises of 4–7 days from major cities. As a result, the most popular cruise destinations in the Pacific are the ones with relative proximity to these Australian ports such as Vanuatu. There are also longer cruises from Australia and New Zealand to countries such as Fiji taking 8–10 days. On longer cruises, some passengers may choose to take only the outward or return section of a cruise, flying the other leg. Cruises to Samoa, Tonga, and the Cook Islands are longer still, and may be part of trans-Pacific or even round the world cruises, with passengers choosing to travel on specific legs and flying to either their origin or destination or both.

All cruise liners have tenders to allow landing where the wharves are too short to allow berthing alongside. The smallest luxury and adventure cruise vessels can berth at many smaller ports and anchor at exotic destinations. Midsized liners up to about 1,500 passengers can berth at the container wharves in the majority of the gateway ports in the Pacific, which cater for vessels up to about 200 m in length. Larger liners can be over 300 m in length and must anchor in sheltered waters and use their tenders to land visiting passengers. Cruise line operators generally prefer to berth alongside when possible for the convenience of passengers, particularly the elderly and infirm, who make up a significant percentage, but this preference is not universal.

The segment with the most critical effect on port operations at gateway ports in the Pacific is the midsized cruise vessels seeking to berth alongside. Most ports are currently multipurpose and these cruise liners use the freight wharves. They take precedence over container vessels as they need to keep closely to tight schedules, particularly for the shorter cruises and may disrupt freight shipping schedules. As such, ports should start considering a provision of a dedicated berth for cruise liners if their overlap with other port operations becomes unbearable.

Ports should also provide separate small vessel berths for cruise liner tenders and good provision will reduce the need for cruise liners to berth alongside. The design of the Provincial Wharf at Alotau in Papua New Guinea has taken this requirement into consideration. It also provides a direct path past the market and war memorials leading along the coast to the town center. This approach is also being adopted at Honiara, where some cruise operators have expressed a preference for operating large vessels, which must be anchored offshore to the main international wharf. Facilities should also be provided at the port entrance for tourist buses, and good landscaping should ensure that the first and last impressions of the visiting town and country are favorable.

- Many ports in the Pacific are multipurpose, catering to container vessels, fishing vessels, and cruise liners simultaneously.
- Cruise liners are given priority over other port traffic, posing a risk of disruption to port operations.

3.6 Consumer Needs and Freight Shipping Patterns

The importance of regular and sufficiently frequent shipping services is a theme frequently brought up by consumers and distributors of imported products in the Pacific. Regular twice monthly from the main Pacific Rim countries, which both supply goods and provide transshipment from Europe and the Americas, were considered necessary, particularly for imported foodstuffs and refrigerated foods.

Until recently, regular twice monthly services have been very rare. An early step in improving regularity was the introduction of fixed shuttle services between New Zealand and Lautoka and Suva in Fiji. This level of service quality has over the last few years been made possible for the majority of other Pacific DMCs through the shipping lines operating consortia offering a well-planned network of routes linking the national gateway ports with the Pacific Rim countries and transshipment ports.

The shipping services providing these linkages are:

- shuttle services such as the New Zealand–Fiji service, and
- loop or string services linking particular Pacific Rim countries and transshipment ports with the various countries in a round service with a regular cycle, which may need more than one vessel.

> Regular shipping services every 2 weeks are often desirable from the perspective of consumers.

The shipping network is almost entirely independent of trans-Pacific shipping routes, as the main trans-Pacific routes do not run close to the Pacific DMCs and volumes are too small to justify calling with a trans-Pacific vessel.

- The regularity of seaborne freight services has seen very substantial improvements recently in the Pacific.
- Freight linkage with major trade partners and transshipment hub in the Pacific Rim countries is critical.

As a general rule in the Pacific, once an efficient regular every 2 weeks schedule linking with ports in the Pacific Rim countries has been established, capacity growth is accommodated by increasing vessel sizes up to the Feedermax size of about 200–220 m LOA with a capacity of about 2,500–3,000 TEUs (but still equipped with ship's gear), thereby obtaining the cost benefits of scale in vessel and port operations.

In smaller countries such as the Cook Islands, Niue, and Tuvalu services are every 3–4 weeks. Better trade linkages may be explored in the future.

3.7 Regional Cooperation and Integration

The level of cooperation among the Pacific DMCs has in recent years been much enhanced largely thanks to regional initiatives such as the Pacific Islands Forum; and governments, donors, and port authorities continue to promote and support cooperation among countries and to explore opportunities for integration at regional and subregional level.

Trade Facilitation

Trade facilitation seeks to promote cross-border movement of goods by reducing the time and cost of such movements. It rests on four core pillars: transparency, simplification, harmonization, and standardization (OECD 2005). These measures enhance the competitiveness of economies, enabling countries to join global value chains in order to sustain economic development. A global survey was conducted in 2017 to assess the status of implementing the World Trade Organization's Trade Facilitation Agreement worldwide. It was found that while the best progress was found in the East and Northeast Asia region (at 73.7%), the Pacific DMCs lag far behind (at 28.2%).[4] Fortunately, support is being provided by development partners to help enhance trade facilitation in various ways.

---

[4] ADB. 2017a. *Trade Facilitation for a More Inclusive and Connected Asia and Pacific Region: Progress and Way Forward.* Manila.

Currently, customs examination in several ports in the Pacific still involves manual inspection of containers. On the other hand, smuggling of illicit drugs and weapons through sophisticated concealment is a growing concern. Catering to increasing trade through the port would thus require enhanced border security and trade facilitation. There is a scope to implement a modern risk-based, intelligent customs management system to strengthen border security. For instance, the Government of New Zealand and ADB are supporting the Apia Port in Samoa to put in place the required hardware (container x-ray scanner) and capacity development program to improve transparency, accountability and most importantly, sustainability of the new customs processes.

Clearance of trade goods typically involve various steps with multiple agencies including, for example, customs, biosecurity, health authority, shipping agents, and customs brokers. Oftentimes in the Pacific, these processes are not integrated, and application, payment, inspection, and document issuance tend to occur in different locations, which can potentially incur unnecessarily large time and cost of trade. The National Single Window concept can bring about efficiencies by providing a common platform through which economic operators and government agencies submit and share information to fulfil the regulatory requirements for custom clearance of trade goods. In Vanuatu, ADB has assisted in developing an implementation plan to roll out the first phase of National Single Window concept, where the recommendations are being implemented by the government with assistance from other development partners. Similarly, in Solomon Islands, ADB provided assistance in developing a one-stop-shop concept at Noro Port to streamline customs process for tuna exports. A new integrated facility is proposed to accommodate and bring together the different government agencies, shipping agents and customs brokers to fast-track customs processes.

Security and Safety

Pacific DMCs are situated on a seaborne route for drug smuggling from Central America to Australia and New Zealand. Local agents, who support these illegal activities, can also be rewarded with drugs. These potentially lead to the growth of drug use in the Pacific DMCs. The larger and more prosperous countries such as Fiji are potentially more vulnerable. Firearms can also be smuggled by the same means. The combination of local drug dealers and weapons in small communities could be deadly.

The implementation of the World Customs Organization Secure and Framework of Standards to Secure and Facilitate Trade (SAFE) call for a comprehensive analysis of the trade supply chain, involving accreditation of all government agencies and the private sector to eliminate any leakages that permit prohibited goods (narcotics, weapons etc.) entering the country. Since the 9/11 event, developing countries, including the Pacific DMCs, have had to comply with the SAFE framework to export to developed countries.

Under international treaties, the Pacific DMCs all have responsibilities for policing their vast EEZs. However, many countries do not have and cannot afford a coast guard or even sufficient patrol boats to cover local coastal needs. Fortunately, the governments of Australia and New Zealand have widely been providing valuable support with reconnaissance aircraft and naval patrol boats.

Ensuring Compliance with International Regulations Environmental Monitoring

Regulatory frameworks have been well established by the International Maritime Organization, requiring the shipping industry to enhance the safety and security of shipping, preventing the marine and atmospheric pollution by ship.[5] However, such regulations assume that individual countries will monitor vessels entering their ports to

---

[5] For more information about International Maritime Organization, refer to their website at http://www.imo.org/en/About/Pages/Default.aspx.

ensure they have the appropriate equipment to comply with international regulations, such as handling of ballast water, smokestack emissions, and solid waste disposal. This is challenging for small ports in the Pacific as they often lack financial resources and technical capacity.

In the case of Apia Port in Samoa, for example, there has been a lack of coordinated effort by the port authority and the relevant stakeholders in managing the environmental and energy efficiency aspects of port operations, thereby undermining their long-term sustainability. ADB is assisting the port authority in bringing together a multiagency technical working group and supporting the development of a green port policy and piloting green port initiatives to promote more environmentally sustainable practices at Apia Port. The pilot serves as a demonstration project, to be replicated for greater benefits to other Pacific DMCs.

Expanding similar actions at a regional level could support Pacific DMCs in ensuring compliance with international regulations of freight and cruise liner vessels in accordance with their duties under the International Maritime Organization frameworks. This will contribute to reducing global emissions of particulates and solid waste including plastics, together with ballast water treatment and offshore release to prevent aggressive species from invading vulnerable marine environments in the Pacific.

3.8 Climate Change Risks

Pacific DMCs are exposed to a wide range of worsening climate-related hazards such as tropical cyclones, floods, droughts, storm surges, and sea level rise.[6] This creates adverse effects on ports and surrounding environment in several ways.

Disruption of Freight and Passenger Loading/Unloading

This is caused by a sea level rise, as a result of the expansion of seawater and melting of glaciers and ice caps due to warmer climate. The usability of wharves is adversely affected as higher sea levels increase the likelihood of overtopping and flooding. Seasonal swell intrusion can also present such operational risks to ports.

Damage to Port Infrastructure

The rise in atmospheric carbon dioxide levels has also increased the amount of carbon dioxide dissolved in seawater, increasing its acidity. As a result, port infrastructure faces increasing risk of corrosion damage. Further, many of the ports in the Pacific are under a constant threat from tropical cyclones, whose frequency and strength climate change also appears to be affecting. According to the most recent models,[7] while cyclone frequencies may remain unaffected, the strengths will increase, accompanied by stronger wind and larger wave.

Damage to Local Fishing and Tourism

Rising water temperature and acidity causes great stress to shellfish and corals, which rely on non-acidic minerals for their strength. This could lead to coral bleaching, and it will become more difficult for marine environment to fully recover from it if the sea acidity and temperature continue to rise. As the corals are the nurseries and refuge for many reef fish and an important tourist attraction, it will have a negative impact on local fishing and tourism.

---

[6] ADB. 2019a. *Building Resilience in The Pacific: How ADB is Addressing Climate Change and Disaster Risks*. Manila.
[7] BoM and CSIRO, 2011. *Climate Change in the Pacific: Scientific Assessment and New Research. Volume 1: Regional Overview*.

Changes in Cyclone Paths and Cyclone Strength

In general, increased temperatures are expected to result in increased strength rather than increased frequency of cyclones and weaker but still destructive severe tropical storms. Paths may also change. These are also affected by the El Niño–Southern Oscillation (ENSO) cycle, and the effects of global warming on ENSO are still unclear.

The design of port infrastructure in the Pacific DMCs needs to take these into consideration. For instance, deck levels will need to be higher and extra corrosion protection will be needed to prevent damages caused by more acidic and warmer seawater in the future. In addition, equipment must be mobile or mounted in a way which allows it to resist overtopping waves. This has been taken into account in the preliminary proposals for the design of new port facilities in Honiara and Noro, Solomon Islands; Alotau, Papua New Guinea; Apia, Samoa; and Nukuʻalofa, Tonga.

For domestic wharves to prepare for the projected sea level rise, the wharf needs to be raised, but raising it too high would compromise efficient use of such infrastructure by vessels with low freeboard. As such, designs may need to be developed allowing the deck to be raised at a later date as was proposed for a provincial wharf in Alotau, Papua New Guinea. A second approach is to increase the use of roll-on/roll-off (ro-ro) vessels for domestic interisland trade since these vessels can use ramps which can be extended inland as sea level rises.

- Ports in the Pacific are particularly vulnerable to climate change, and associated risks are increasing.
- At the same time, the port itself can harm surrounding environment, particularly during the expansion.

Ports in the Pacific need to be better climate-proofed and mitigate any impact caused to the surrounding environment.

3.9 Exposure to Natural Hazards

Pacific DMCs are vulnerable to different kinds of natural hazards.

An average of one to two tropical cyclones was recorded in the Pacific per year from 1988 to 2017.[8] Tropical cyclones pose risk to port infrastructure and their tracks vary with ENSO.

The Pacific region has a number of active and dormant volcanoes, which are local risks. The most serious occurrence in recent times was Rabaul in Papua New Guinea in 1994, when the Tavuvur eruption destroyed the airport and old town. Overall, the region is located on one of the most active segments of the so-called Pacific Ring of Fire, the arc of seismic faults, where most of the world's earthquakes activity occur. The earthquakes themselves produce severe physical damage, but it can also trigger other types of natural hazards such as tsunamis. They can inundate and damage towns and ports on which victims rely for emergency relief. Mega-tsunamis could also be created by the collapse of the underwater slopes of giant volcanoes.

It is therefore critical for the Pacific DMCs to improve resilience to these disasters, as they are situated in one of the most disaster-prone geographical area. However, there are often barriers to building stronger resilience in the

---

[8] SPEArTC (http://apdrc.soest.hawaii.edu/projects/speartc/) and Diamond, H.J., A.M. Lorrey, K.R. Knapp, and D.H. Levinson, 2012. *Development of an enhanced tropical cyclone tracks database for the southwest Pacific from 1840–2011*. International Journal of Climatology, 32: 2240–2250. DOI:10.1002/joc.2412.

region. These include (i) inadequate public awareness; (ii) inadequate institutional systems and capacity to plan; (iii) limited training and technology transfer on adaptation and mitigation technologies; and (iv) lack of financial resources to undertake assessment, planning, and adaptation efforts.

It would be vital in the short term for Pacific DMCs to put in place national disaster preparedness plans that encompass the respective types of disasters that they are exposed to. It must be designed to provide the best possible early warning of potential natural hazards to the target population and ensure that the relevant personnel are trained in the actions needed to save lives during and in the aftermath of a disaster.

Not only as a main point of international trade activities, but the gateway ports in the Pacific also tend to play a lifeline function in the aftermath of a disaster by supporting subsequent relief efforts. Therefore, an important consideration in port design is to ensure the basic infrastructure and facilities can withstand the impacts of the disaster so that the port remains operational in the immediate aftermath of such occurrence. This is crucial to ensure access to emergency aid and supply of daily necessities to the mainland or smaller islands, some of which may have been almost wiped out by a cyclone wave or tsunami. Further, ports must have their own disaster preparedness plan, which are linked to the national disaster preparedness plans. This is critical to mitigate the residual risks that cannot be mitigated with structural measures.

Such approaches are increasingly being adopted by the port renewal and expansion plans in the Pacific. The Alotau Wharf in Papua New Guinea, for instance, is designed not to be overwhelmed by cyclone waves without serious damage and to reopen as soon as the storm passes. Any future improvements to the Alofi Wharf in Niue must take account of cyclone waves up to 35 m high over the entire port area and the coastal road behind it, so all vital equipment must be mobile. At the Honiara Port in Solomon Islands, a wharf has been selected as the lifeline wharf and its design checked to the more rigorous standards required for a lifeline structure.

- Pacific DMCs are situated in one of the most disaster-prone geographical areas.
- Ports are expected to function as "lifeline" facilities and need to be resilient

Formulating their own disaster preparedness plan linked to the national strategy is key for Pacific ports to be disaster resilient.

3.10 Common Development Issues

Many Pacific DMC ports have their origin in multipurpose ports, located in the centers of the national capitals. They served both international and domestic freight and passenger services as well as local commercial and subsistence fishing. However, trade expansion and containerization of last few decades have changed port infrastructure and operational requirements progressively.

Managing the Transition from Break-Bulk General Cargo to Container Shipments

The transition from break–bulk general cargo to container shipments has meant that ports have had to adapt their infrastructure. Loose cargo requires covered warehousing close to the berth to minimize the transit distances between the loading and unloading cranes and the storage facilities. Conversely, the handling of containers requires large open storage areas with much greater surfacing strength to accommodate specialized heavy handling equipment and high container stacking levels. The net result is that several of the ports are suffering from increasing congestion due to the overall lack of storage capacity within the existing port boundaries, impeded access to backland storage areas, and surfacing problems caused by the application of heavy container handling machinery.

Arising Needs for Terminal Separation

As international trade and the cruise industry have expanded, the international vessels have increased in size and have required separate wharves from those serving fishing boats and smaller domestic vessels. As a result, the multipurpose wharves have been replaced by separate facilities designed for a specific purpose. Local fishing boats have usually been the first to move to separate wharves, often associated with landside fish markets.

The second stage has usually been the separation of the domestic wharves. Domestic vessels provide essential local services, particularly in nations consisting of extended island clusters and archipelagos. They usually carry both passengers and freight, which need careful landside traffic planning for safety and efficiency. Increasingly, there has been a need for ro-ro ramps to cater for freight and commuter traffic between adjacent islands.

A third development has been moving fuel tanker facilities out of the port area. Most tanker berths are now swinging mooring points with undersea pipelines connecting to tanks or specialized tanker berths.

Figure 3.1 sets out the typical stages in a transition from multipurpose port to a full separation of port operations.

Figure 3.1: Typical Transition of a Multipurpose Port in the Pacific

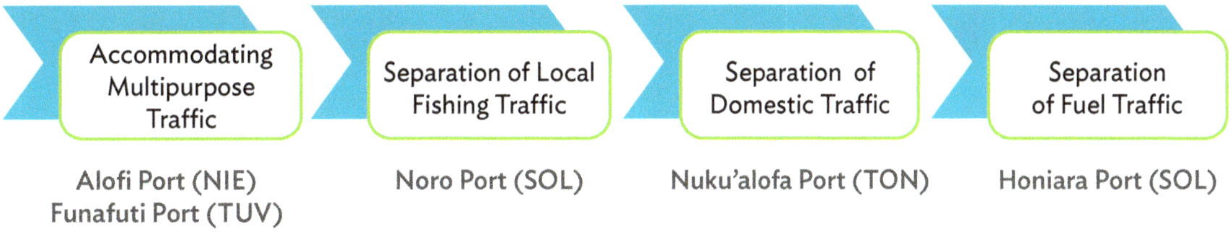

Accommodating Multipurpose Traffic	Separation of Local Fishing Traffic	Separation of Domestic Traffic	Separation of Fuel Traffic
Alofi Port (NIE) Funafuti Port (TUV)	Noro Port (SOL)	Nuku'alofa Port (TON)	Honiara Port (SOL)

NIE = Niue, SOL = Solomon Islands, TON = Tonga, TUV = Tuvalu.
Source: Asian Development Bank (Pacific Department).

The situation at some ports is further compounded by the growth in tourism, especially during the December–March peak cruising period. Passenger liners have priority and require extensive quay space. This means the quay becomes inoperable for freight activities, with cargo vessels being delayed as they have to vacate berths.

As a result, there is increasing pressure to separate passenger and freight operations, particularly when callings rise above once per week. Passenger traffic needs to be retained in the city area, whereas freight can be moved outside. Such a major transition takes time and is expensive because of the need for significant changes in infrastructure. Evidence of this trend are Nuku'alofa in Tonga, where the freight operations are being transferred to new sites and the passenger traffic being retained at the city location.

Outdated Port Infrastructure

The wharves built in the 1970s, when trade began to expand, are reaching the end of their economic lives under the design codes of that time. Some wharves can no longer accommodate container vessels alongside as their size now exceed the originally designed draught. Substantial rehabilitation or reconstruction may be needed to bring them back to operable and safe standards, and to cope with the increased demands on the port. As mentioned in earlier chapters, future port rehabilitation or upgrades should also incorporate earthquake-resilient design wherever applicable.

Large parts of the existing yards are typically unsuitable for stacking laden containers other than empty ones as they were most often designed to accommodate a need for low load cargo only, which was a standard freight type when the expansion was done. To accommodate additional container demand, the container yards could be strengthened to carry higher loads to allow stacking laden containers up to four containers height. In the short term, clearing of the warehousing on the berths previously required for loose general cargo provides extra storage space and an opportunity to improve yard layout and circulation.

Optimizing Container Handling Equipment

In planning for port expansion, the nature of the container handling equipment needed should also be considered.

Large terminals use large rail-mounted ship-to-shore cranes, which can transfer up to 50 TEUs per hour. The rule of thumb is that for the efficient and cost-effective use of modern rail-mounted ship-to-shore gantry cranes, terminals require a minimum of about one crane per 120 m of quay face each handling about 140,000 or more TEUs per year. As such, a minimum straight quay length of 600 m for two berths would require a minimum of five cranes and would have a capacity in excess of 700,000 TEUs per year. It would not be cost-effective to install them until throughput rose to roughly 400,000 TEUs per year.

On the other hand, small ports such as the majority of those in the Pacific tend to rely on cranes carried on board the vessels. This has the additional advantage that crane maintenance can take place at the vessel's home port, where skilled maintenance engineers and spares are easily available. This approach works well with most ports at the moment, but the ship's gear cranes can only handle approximately 16 TEUs per hour. This means they cannot by themselves handle throughputs of over about 60,000 TEUs per year using only the ships cranes without congestion.

The solution would be to supplement them with mobile harbor cranes (MHCs). These are mobile tower cranes, which extend spreaders and lift their wheels to provide stability while lifting containers and can be positioned flexibly to work jointly with the ships own cranes. They can transfer about 30 TEUs per hour, less than rail-mounted cranes but a lot more than ships gear cranes and ensure that the larger vessels can transfer about 60 TEUs per hour. MHCs may also be used in smaller ports which are served mainly by vessels with no ships gear.

As for transporting goods within the port boundary, reach stackers can provide a more flexible solution in smaller yards, where containers are stacked close to the quay face. Where the yard area is further away from the quay face, however, the disadvantages become more prominent. These become an expensive means of moving the containers within the terminal, and also impose higher loading on the pavement.

For larger yards, a combination of tugs and trailers with top lifters, possibly in combination with some reach stackers, may be more efficient and cost-effective. A significant factor in the Pacific is the high percentage of exported empty containers, which have a longer dwell time in the yard. This points to the use of dedicated empty containers stacks with higher stacking heights.

Increased downtime of container handling equipment tends to be a familiar problem worldwide, but particularly acute to the remote ports in the Pacific, where there is often a shortage of the expertise needed to service, maintain, and repair such sophisticated equipment, as well as access to ongoing funding for spares parts and repairs. The increase in container operations that requires the use of evermore sophisticated handling equipment and IT systems creates a pressing need for specialized resources to support these changes.

Short-/Long-Term Solutions and Opportunities

There is no one-size-fits-all solution to these common port development issues. However, in a resource-constrained environment, an incremental approach may be considered to manage increased port demand in a sustainable manner.

Prior to making large investments in expansion plans, it would be prudent to first explore cost-effective solutions to enhance operational efficiency and capacity gains of the existing port. This could include options discussed earlier, such as reviewing the internal operations of the existing port and bringing in additional equipment such as MHCs. In doing so, it is important to ensure regular maintenance of existing and new assets can be sustained to ensure reliability and sustained productivity. Such interventions would tend to minimize land and environmental issues, as compared to an option to relocate the port operation immediately.

Should additional land area be required, reclamation or superstructure reconfiguration may be considered, such as the removal of buildings. The latter can provide extra storage capacity. This is the situation at Lautoka in Fiji and Apia in Samoa. The development of customs transit systems could also help in expanding the use of off-port processing facilities such as inland container depots and container freight stations. These facilities help reduce dwell times within the port, thus enabling higher utilization of each ground storage slot within the terminal, thereby enhancing operational efficiency. Cruise liner facilities are best retained in the town center if possible, but designs such as finger jetties combined with mooring dolphins may reduce costs and land-take.

In the medium term, separating or providing additional facilities for cruise vessels, tankers, international container vessels, domestic shipping (increasingly ro-ro), and fishing vessels can mitigate delays when higher-priority vessels occupy a single multipurpose wharf.

When land is no longer available in the town center area, relocating container facilities may be considered. Social and environmental impacts need to be carefully assessed, particularly when developing greenfield ports. Since relocation is often an expensive option, it is critical to assess the financial viability and bankability of such a large-scale investment. This should be underpinned by credible and robust port demand forecasts. Given the large-scale and complex nature of such a project, a longer preparation time would be required to plan, design, and secure funding for implementation.

Above all, apart from hard infrastructure, soft infrastructure needs to be in place to ensure the smooth integration of the multitude of processes in a port. Procedures for customs, biosecurity, and food quarantine should be streamlined, supported by reliable systems and equipment. Personnel training and support need to be put in place to ensure the system is operated smoothly.

Smarter Solutions to Ports in the Pacific

Considering the specific characteristics of the Pacific, not all but some of the smart port solutions that are effective in other parts of the world may work in the Pacific. Below is an overview of typical smart port solutions with some views on its applicability in the Pacific context.

Energy Efficiency

Solutions like solar or wind energy can be easily implemented as well as LED lighting for the terminals.

Operational Efficiency

There could be potential opportunities to improve operational efficiency using new technologies in the Pacific. Implementing digital systems to measure performance and to identify bottlenecks in the port operations seem very much relevant in the Pacific context.

Smart Asset Management

Smart asset management is applicable and can help to reduce the operational expenditures in the Pacific context, but it should be considered that the amount of investment and type of system that is selected is in line with the complexity of the assets in the port.

Safety and Security

Any technology that will improve the safety of individuals and the security of the cargo could be applied in the Pacific context. Again, investments in digital solutions should be in line with the safety and security that is aimed for. For instance, a closed circuit television or CCTV system may help to supplement and improve the terminal security and reduce the need for manual security rounds.

Long-Term Port Connectivity

The end goal of the implementation of smart ports solutions is to connect users within the port and its hinterland, followed by connectivity between different ports. This could definitely be a (long-term) objective for the Pacific to reduce transport costs for the region.

A Range of Opportunities for Private Sector Engagement

The private sector has always been actively involved in port affairs. The land and water transport services that use the ports often involve the private sector. Nearly all of the cargo shipped through ports is privately owned. The private sector provides an array of complementary trade facilitation and logistics services for this cargo. Within the confines of the public port, cargo owners, forwarders, and ship agents actively participate in decisions concerning the handling and storage of cargo and development of commonly used facilities.[9]

The challenges ports are facing in the Pacific create opportunities for private sector involvement and active participation. There is a wide spectrum of private sector involvement from small to large scale, which has already manifested in the region, and more is expected to occur in coordination with port authorities and local governments. Some examples of recent private sector participation in addressing operational and capacity constraints include:

---

[9] ADB. 2000. *Developing Best Practices for Promoting Private Sector Investment in Infrastructure: Ports.* Manila.

- Maersk shipping line's infrastructure investments at Noro Port to support expanded fishing processing and export operations;
- stevedore operations, such as in Apia Port in Samoa; and
- build, operate, and transfer concession model at Tibar Bay in Timor-Leste.

4 Recent Asian Development Bank Approaches in Project Development

Strategy 2030 sets the course for ADB to respond effectively to the current challenges in the Pacific.

The Pacific Approach[10] is closely aligned with the strategic priorities of ADB's Strategy 2030.[11] Consistent with global initiatives, the Pacific Approach supports national efforts toward the Sustainable Development Goals (SDGs) and the achievement of the 2030 Agenda for Sustainable Development.

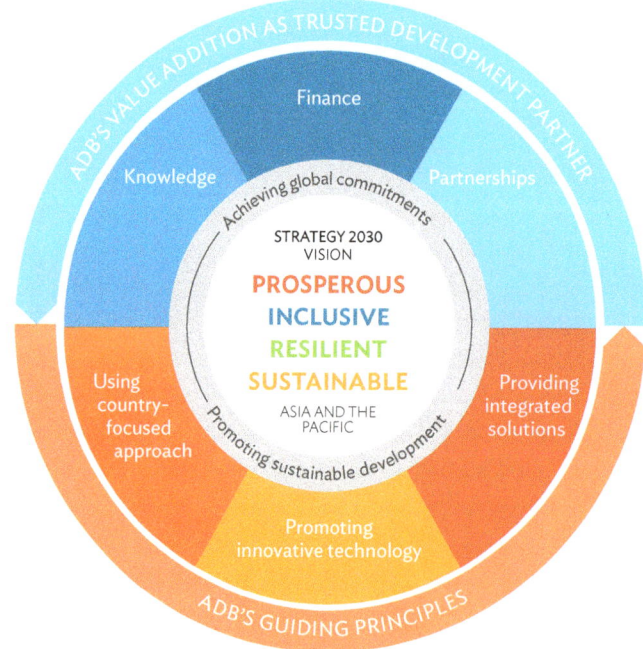

Figure 4.1: Asian Development Bank Strategy 2030

Source: Asian Development Bank.

New SDGs to which ADB is well placed to contribute include climate change action (SDG 13) and conservation and sustainable use of oceans and marine resources (SDG 14)—goals that the Small Island Developing States group was instrumental in forging. Inclusive economic growth (SDG 8) and building capable, responsive institutions (SDG 16)

---

[10] *The Pacific Approach, 2016–2020* (ADB. 2017b) serves as the operational framework of ADB for the Pacific region and as the country partnership strategy for the 11 smaller Pacific island countries—the Cook Islands, Kiribati, the Marshall Islands, the Federated States of Micronesia, Nauru, Palau, Samoa, Solomon Islands, Tonga, Tuvalu, and Vanuatu.
[11] ADB. 2018. *Strategy 2030*. Manila.

are also central to ADB's Pacific Approach. ADB's core operations support progress toward ending poverty in all its forms (SDG 1); achieving gender equality and empowering women and girls (SDG 5); providing universal access to water and sanitation (SDG 6) and modern energy (SDG 7); building resilient infrastructure (SDG 9); and promoting sustained and inclusive economic growth, full productive employment, and decent work (SDG 8).

Seven operational priorities set out in ADB Strategy 2030 plus Healthy Oceans and Sustainable Blue Economies,[12] which is relevant to the operations in the maritime sector, are summarized in Box 5:

Box 5: Operational Priorities

Addressing remaining poverty and reducing inequalities

The Asian Development Bank (ADB) will increase the emphasis on human development and social inclusion to address the non-income dimensions of poverty. It will help facilitate quality job creation, including by small and medium-sized enterprises and inclusive businesses. ADB will support developing member countries (DMCs) to improve education and training outcomes, achieve better health for all, and strengthen social protection systems and service delivery for those in need.

Accelerating progress in gender equality

ADB will support targeted operations to empower women and girls, gender mainstreaming that directly narrows gender gaps, and operations with some gender elements that incorporate a few gender equality actions in the design and implementation of ADB projects and programs. At least 75% of the number of ADB's committed operations (on a 3-year rolling average, including sovereign and nonsovereign operations) will promote gender equality by 2030.

Tackling climate change, building climate and disaster resilience, and enhancing environmental sustainability

ADB will scale up support in these areas. ADB will ensure that 75% of the number of its committed operations (on a 3-year rolling average, including sovereign and nonsovereign operations) will be supporting climate change mitigation and adaptation by 2030. Climate finance from ADB's own resources will reach $80 billion cumulatively from 2019 to 2030.

Making cities more livable

ADB will provide integrated solutions to help build livable cities that are green, competitive, resilient, and inclusive. It will pursue crosscutting projects to promote urban health, urban mobility, gender equality, and environmental sustainability. ADB will help cities explore new and expand existing sources of funding, enhance inclusive and participatory urban planning, and integrate climate resilience and disaster risk management considerations into urban planning processes.

Promoting rural development and food security

ADB will support efforts to improve market connectivity and agricultural value chain linkages. It will help DMCs increase agricultural productivity and food security by boosting farm and nonfarm incomes, promoting the adoption of advanced technologies and climate-smart agricultural practices, and supporting the improvement of natural resource management standards. It will also help DMCs enhance food safety.

continued on next page

---

[12] ADB. 2019b. *Action Plan for Healthy Oceans*. Manila.

Box 5 *continued*

Strengthening governance and institutional capacity
ADB will support public management reforms to help DMCs improve governance and create an enabling environment for sustainable growth. It will help countries build resilience and respond to economic shocks, strengthen service delivery, and improve capacity and standards. ADB will uphold environmental and social safeguards, adhere to fiduciary standards, and implement anticorruption measures in all its projects and programs.

Fostering regional cooperation and integration
ADB will enhance connectivity in the region and the competitiveness of DMCs. It will increase support for regional public goods and collective actions to mitigate cross-border risks such as climate change, pollution, energy and water security, and communicable and infectious diseases. ADB will also enhance financial sector cooperation and strengthen subregional initiatives, including through facilitating knowledge sharing and collaboration, and working with emerging initiatives.

Healthy Oceans and Sustainable Blue Economies
ADB will support the protection and restoration of marine ecosystems and promote inclusive livelihood opportunities. Supporting ADB's DMCs to improve ocean health and achieve Sustainable Development Goal 14: Life Below Water ensures the livelihoods, health, resiliency, and food security of billions of people in the region.

4.1 Recent Challenges in Pacific Ports

Five case studies have been selected to showcase unique challenges small ports in the Pacific face, and how ADB is supporting Pacific DMCs to overcome them.

Climate Proofing Alotau Provincial Wharf in Papua New Guinea

The Building Resilience to Climate Change Project is strengthening the capacity of communities, government agencies, and civil society to plan for and respond to the effects of climate change. A key component of the project is to climate proof the provincial wharf at Alotau, which is the capital of Milne Bay Province.

The wharf is vulnerable to the adverse effects of climate change, especially sea level rise and increasingly intensive storm surges. As such, it was essential that the replacement wharf is appropriately climate-proofed. In addition to the installation of stronger foundations, the deck level was proposed to be raised by 30 centimeters (cm) initially, which is the forecast future sea level rise in the period to 2070 and is the maximum feasible elevation for existing low-freeboard vessels.

Typical provincial vessel (photo by ADB).

The proposed design at the same time left flexibility for deck level to be raised by a further 50 cm at a low cost if sea level rise rate accelerates in the future. This two-stage adaptive approach to the adverse effect of climate change was suggested to maximize functionality and operability of the wharf during its service life. The second elevation of the wharf would be triggered as and when further sea level rise begins to impact efficient and safe wharf operations.

Stepped landings are also designed on the side of the wharf to provide further accessibility for a full range of vessel sizes and tidal conditions.

ADB Operational Priorities behind the Project

 **The project directly benefits the poor as it seeks to improve accessibility for the low-income population residing in the remote outer islands, to the provincial town of Alotau.**

 **The proposed climate-resilient wharf design serves as a prototype with strong demonstration potential for replication across other, similar coastal infrastructure assets.**

 **Gender-responsive design features were incorporated in the proposed design of the provincial wharf.**

Outer Islands Maritime Infrastructure Project Phase 2 in Tuvalu

The Outer Island Maritime Infrastructure Project is helping Tuvalu overcome connectivity constraints by improving maritime facilities on three outer islands, and by building government capacity to plan, implement, and maintain transport infrastructure. The project is increasing access to the outer islands by (i) constructing a new harbor on Nukulaelae and rehabilitating boat ramps on Nanumaga and Niutao; (ii) building capacity to operate and maintain assets; and (iii) developing a transport sector master plan for further sequenced investments, with a view toward promoting economic activity through fisheries and tourism.

Prior to the project, there were no docking facilities available at Niutao harbor to accommodate the government ships carrying domestic passengers and freight. The wind and current run along the exposed reef and a very steep drop into deep water means that the interisland vessel cannot anchor offshore and must maintain its position under motor while passengers and goods are transferred in small powered flat-bottomed workboats which land on the reef. Passenger transfer is very laborious and cargo, the elderly and infirm in wheelchairs are manually handled, posing serious safety risks and operational inefficiency.

Current cargo transfer operation (photo by ADB).

Boat harbor and related facilities are needed to improve travel safety and cargo shipping services.

ADB Operational Priorities behind the Project

The upgraded maritime infrastructure will enhance connectivity and maritime safety between Niutao and the main island of Funafuti. This is critical to sustaining economic activities, particularly among small business owners, and reducing migration from the outer islands to Funafuti.

The project will incorporate higher standards of climate resilience in the maritime facilities, thereby enhancing safety and efficiency of vessel operations.

Apia Port Development Project in Samoa

Apia Port operates as a singular international gateway for nearly 100% of all physical freight movements in and out of Samoa. The port supports the entire country's consumer demand for essential imported commodities and provides the gateway for primary export products to regional and global markets. However, its operations are hindered by seasonal and long-period swell conditions and the port faces increasing risks from natural hazards.

The project is thus designed to enhance the climate and disaster resilience of the port, as well as enhance border security and trade facilitation through effective border management. The core components include (i) rehabilitation of the existing breakwater to provide better protection for the port operation, (ii) upgrade terminal infrastructure to improve operation standards, (iii) installation of new customs examination facility including x-ray scanner to secure and facilitate global trade and prevent illegal arms imports, and (iv) replacement of the existing older tugboat to ensure continued safe port operations.

Current Berth Operation (photo by ADB).

ADB Operational Priorities behind the Project

 Green port initiatives will be implemented in accordance with international best practices. Impacts of port operations on women in the local communities will be addressed. Greater participation of women employees will be promoted to undertake technical and managerial roles.

 The upgraded customs management facilities will enable the government to implement a modern risk-based intelligent customs management system. This would enhance border security and trade facilitation at Apia Port.

 The reconstruction of the existing breakwater, implementation of a multihazard disaster preparedness plan and new tugboat will provide a boost to improve safety of port operations, and climate and disaster resilience of Apia Port.

Developing Noro Port Development Project in Solomon Islands

Noro lies on the western coast of New Georgia Island. It is a regional transport and fishing hub and the second international port of entry for Solomon Islands and is located in a sheltered deepwater inlet. Productive tuna fishing areas in the adjacent waters makes Noro as a strategically important port for fish exporting, attracting private investment.

In anticipation of further expansion of the fishing industry as a result of the partnership Solomon Islands Ports Authority (SIPA) formed with private business partners recently, a technical assessment was undertaken to help SIPA review the short- to medium-term investment requirements, and develop strategic expansion plan for Noro Port to cater to additional fish export demands.

Fish processing at Noro (photo by ADB).

Currently, operations at Noro Port are hindered by frequent calls made by domestic vessels, disrupting efficient fish unloading operation and posing biosecurity risk to export fish products. The technical assessment explored options of construction of a separate jetty for domestic vessels was thus proposed to attract more distant water fishing vessels from destinations such as Japan, the Republic of Korea, and Taipei,China.

The high cost of networked utilities is another concern particularly for the shipping line, who make regular calls to Noro Port to export fish products using refrigerated containers. If the fish export volume increases as envisaged, so does the electricity demands. The feasibility of introducing renewable energy source at Noro was thus also assessed, and technical investment options comprised of solar, battery storage, and diesel gensets were developed.

ADB Operational Priorities behind the Project

 **Growth in the fishing industry will provide sustainable local employment. Further expansion of the fishing industry may generate spin-off businesses in consumer retail, wholesale, banking, fuel sales, transport, as well as a fresh produce market, bringing further economic opportunities to the local population.**

 **SIPA aims to improve the efficiency and carbon footprint of the Noro Port through captive solar power generation. This initiative will help SIPA make progress toward its vision of transforming Noro Port into a carbon-neutral port by 2030. A proposed local microgrid system has the potential to reduce carbon dioxide, carbon monoxide, particulate matter, nitrogen oxide, and sulfur oxide emissions by 32% during the first year of operation.**

 **The proposed investment will facilitate the growth in international trade and support the associated growth in domestic cargo movements at Noro Port. It will improve the regional integrity of Noro Port by maximizing operational efficiency and providing dedicated wharfage to growing domestic vessel traffic. It also leaves room for future wharf extension to maximize flexibility of land use.**

Developing Alofi Wharf Project in Niue

Airfreight connections are limited in Niue, as they are dependent on load capacity being available on each twice weekly service to and from Auckland. During the peak tourist season, airfreight capacity is often nonexistent. As such, the population is heavily reliant on maritime transport and such infrastructure is their lifeline.

Since it was constructed in the 1930s, the primary international maritime terminal in Niue has been Sir Robert's Wharf in Alofi, the capital. In the early years, containers were landed directly at the wharf from small general cargo and later small container vessels, but the vessels making regular calls have now become too large to berth alongside. Instead, they are moored Mediterranean style, anchored offshore and moored to the wharf with a quick release hook. Cargo is transferred onshore by a barge and work boat. The wharf is exposed to the ocean swells during the wet season, and thus often damaged during bad weather, requiring repair and further limiting operations.

Given these challenges, the rationale for a port investment in Niue was assessed, considering existing and expected traffic and quality and size of current infrastructure.

Wave overtopping at Sir Robert's Wharf (photo by ADB).

There are several interventions, which would improve efficiency and safety of port operations, and infrastructure resilience both on the landslide and on the marine side. Design concepts for improvement of Niue's maritime infrastructure, with focus on developments of the Sir Robert's Wharf, have been developed for port development and other maritime facilities to simplify port operation, increase efficiency, and make the wharf more resilient to the anticipated effects of climate change.

ADB Operational Priorities behind the Project

 Options for a dedicated container and boat wash down facilities with water catchment systems at the container yard and the container depot were explored to mitigate potential impacts to the marine habitat.

 Since Cyclone Heta damaged relevant facilities in 2004, all fuel has been imported in tanktainers, posing environmental risk of oil spillage. Reducing the volumes of oil imports to cut down the trade deficit and atmospheric emissions by developing solar sources is already in progress, but improving the controls for tanktainer handling is also critical. This was addressed in the study for further consideration by the government.

 Tourism is Niue's primary industry, and of growing importance to the economy as an "invisible" export balancing the trade deficit. However, with a population of 1,600 and a workforce of around 800 people, maintaining the current rate of growth will not be sustainable. Islanders' aspiration for sustainable tourism and fisheries were also noted during the stakeholder consultation, and this was fully incorporated into the development concepts.

Appendix: Gateway Seaports Trade Outlook

Further information on seaport trade forecasts in the selected Pacific developing member countries (DMCs) is provided below.

A1.1 Fiji

Suva Port is the next largest port in the Pacific after Lae Port in Papua New Guinea. It has begun to develop an international transshipment capacity in recent years, in part due to the Pacific Direct Line services from Fiji to neighboring islands, which make use of Fiji as a transshipment hub. Due to the longer dwell time of transshipment containers, further growth in the transshipment market at Fiji would require expansion of the current port or relocation to a new facility, the location of which is still to be determined. Suva will remain primarily a container import terminal with the modest growth in recent years forecast to continue.

Lautoka Port has a large share of full export twenty-foot equivalent units (TEUs) compared to other ports in the Pacific. This is primarily due to Fiji Water exports, which use Lautoka. There remain strong growth prospects for this product, but the port is highly reliant on one customer, which makes long-term estimates of growth problematic and there is a risk of a change in trend. Lautoka has increased the number of full container imports in recent years.

A1.2 Papua New Guinea

Papua New Guinea has experienced a sustained period of high investment and infrastructure construction over the past decade. With the completion of the Papua New Guinea Liquefied Natural Gas (LNG) project in 2014, the development of all major construction projects has slowed. This has led to reduced employment and spending in the economy and a corresponding slowdown in trade volumes. In terms of containerized trade, Port Moresby has been particularly affected with reduced container volumes since 2013, though Lae Port has continued to grow albeit at a slower rate since 2012.

The historical trade at Port Moresby was largely driven by government spending and is forecast to grow in line with gross domestic product (GDP) growth going forward. Lae Port, which is the gateway to the resource and agriculturally rich Central Highlands, will continue to be the main port for the country. Although low resource prices have delayed plans for further LNG projects, these are likely to be developed in the next decade and Lae Port should benefit from associated trade. Due to its location, it is likely to continue to grow at a faster rate than the other international ports in Papua New Guinea. Current throughput is expected to roughly double in the next 20 years.

Due to the additional capacity provided by the Lae Tidal Basin Phase I development and the new port facility at Motukea Port Moresby, there is some opportunity for both Port Moresby and Lae to develop as transshipment hubs for the Pacific region. Consultations with the main shipping lines suggest that the major crossover points for Pacific services are Lae, Moresby, Noumea, and Suva, and transshipment activities will continue to grow at all these ports, albeit in some cases from a low base. Due to the diverse range of shipping services in the region, it is unlikely that any of these locations will become a dominant single hub. For this reason, transshipment is forecast to continue to grow in line with regional trade growth both at Lae and Moresby (although a 10%–20% jump in transshipment when Motukea is fully operational is possible).

Papua New Guinea is the only Pacific DMC with large-scale domestic container shipping. Lae Port, in particular, acts as a hub for the smaller ports in the north and east of Papua New Guinea. The large number of empty TEU imports at Lae are primarily domestic rather than international as full containers of goods are exported to the regions and these empty containers come back through Lae as imports.

A1.3 Samoa

Like most of the Pacific DMC ports, Apia is dominated by full container imports and empty exports. The majority of exports are refrigerated containers exporting frozen fish, which are landed on the wharf and loaded directly into 40-foot (ft) containers. In 2016, export trade suffered from the closure of the Yazaki EDS, which prepared wiring harnesses for the Australian motor industry following the closure of the facilities operated by the two main manufacturers in Australia, General Motors and Ford.

As the port volume is heavily reliant on import containers, future growth is reliant on the growth in local incomes in order to support the country's trade imbalance. Currently remittances, of both money and goods, support a large proportion of the trade imbalance. It is debatable if these will continue at current levels as remittances often slow down once the second generation of emigrants become the main income earners. Economic factors also point to slow trade growth over the coming years as real GDP per capita has been flat for the last 4 years and population growth is less than 1% per annum tax adjustments may benefit exports, but they are less likely to benefit imports.

There has been strong growth in container volumes in recent years caused by the structural shift toward containerization and the high level of remittances supporting import growth overall. However, this is unlikely to continue as the containerization shift is largely complete and remittance growth may falter.

Although there is a base level of transshipment containers at Apia Port currently, none of the shipping lines interviewed indicated any likelihood of expansion of this trade.

A1.4 Timor-Leste

In 2013, non-oil GDP growth slowed, largely as a result of a decrease in government capital expenditure associated with the completion of the Hera Power Plant project. This impacted Dili Port through a reduction in imports of construction material and also a decrease of local labor demand, which caused lower income levels and, in turn, a decreasing demand for import of consumption items. Since the parliamentary election in 2007, container throughput at Dili Port in Timor-Leste accelerated and more than doubled in the 5-year period to 2012. Since then container trade growth has been more variable. Looking forward, other developments which may reduce future imports at Dili Port are the construction of a cement bagging facility, which will take bulk product directly from its own jetty and thus reduce the need for imported bagged cement, and the construction of a beer, soft drink, and water bottling plant in Dili, which will greatly reduce the amount of imported beverages. Exports are limited mostly to coffee and while some growth can be expected, the port will continue to be dominated by imports.

The Timor-Leste economy is heavily reliant on government spending, which is in turn reliant on the Petroleum Fund for the majority of government revenues. Lower than expected oil and gas revenues due to the lower oil price in recent years have put pressure on the government to reduce outflows from the fund to ensure long-term sustainability. This has led to a downgrade of future growth assumptions by the International Monetary Fund.[1] Nonetheless, with continued high population growth and ongoing plans for government-led infrastructure development, the economy is expected to continue to grow at around 5% per annum in the medium term. This is expected to support strong growth in container volumes, although not at rates that were seen pre-2013.

In June 2016, French port operator Bolloré was awarded the concession contract to develop the new international terminal at Tibar Bay west of Dili. Press reports at that time indicated that the port is anticipated to be operational by 2020 and to have an annual capacity of 350,000 TEUs per year. For the purpose of the forecasts, this will not influence import and export demand significantly. It will however provide increased capacity, which is likely to be required at some point in the next decade, as the existing facility is heavily constrained for both berth and yard space.

A1.4 Tonga

The breakdown of container traffic at Nuku'alofa Port is typical of many Pacific DMCs. Imports are dominant due to the lack of local manufacturing. Foodstuffs, machinery, and transport equipment are the main import commodities. Tonga has some exports of agricultural products (squash, vanilla bean) and fish; however, volumes are low.

Despite sluggish economic growth in the past decade, Nuku'alofa Port has experienced strong growth in container volumes since 2011. The reasons were a succession of aid projects requiring imports of goods and materials, following which the damage created by Typhoon Gita led to a further wave of both aid and domestic reconstruction projects, leading to further imports. The country's large trade deficit has been supported by international development assistance and a high level of remittances (personal remittances were equivalent to 26% of GDP in 2015).[2] As such, the same levels of container volume increase over the last decade are not likely to be sustainable in the long term.

A1.5 Vanuatu

Vanuatu's economy is heavily reliant on the tourism industry, with tourism receipts corresponding to 73% of the total value of exports in 2014 (footnote 2). Other domestic industries are relatively undeveloped with agriculture being primarily subsistence-based. The country has a limited agricultural export base with beef and coffee being the two major export commodities. The service focus of the economy is reflected in the container volumes at Port Vila of its heavy reliance on imports.

The other main industry in Vanuatu, especially in the Port Vila region, is construction. Primarily this is focused on the tourism industry, but in recent years there have also been a number of large urban development projects undertaken including:

---

[1] International Monetary Fund. *IMF Country Report No.16/183*.
[2] World Bank Development Indicators. Available at https://databank.worldbank.org/source/world-development-indicators

- New International Multimodal Port—Port Vila;
- Road Reconstruction from Bauerfield Airport to Port Vila Sea Port; and
- Port Vila Seafront Promenade.

These projects have caused a short-term spike in trade volumes. This is expected to continue in the short term, but indications from local shipping agents suggest that the beneficial effect will fade out over time and that volumes will begin to revert to the long-term trend. Further long-term growth in container volumes will be enabled by the development of a new port facility, but will require continued growth in the tourism industry, as well as a long-term uplift in local incomes. Excluding the short-term impact of the current construction boom, container volumes are forecast to increase around 100% across the 20-year forecast period.

References

Asian Development Bank (ADB). 2019a. *Building Resilience in The Pacific: How ADB is Addressing Climate Change and Disaster Risks*. Manila.

ADB. 2019b. *Action Plan for Healthy Oceans*. Manila

ADB. 2018. *Strategy 2030*. Manila.

ADB. 2017a. *Trade Facilitation for a More Inclusive and Connected Asia and Pacific Region: Progress and Way Forward*. Manila.

ADB. 2017b. *Pacific Approach 2016 – 2020*. Manila.

ADB. 2000. *Developing Best Practices for Promoting Private Sector Investment in Infrastructure: Ports*. Manila

Australian Bureau of Meteorology (BoM) and Commonwealth Scientific and Industrial Research Organisation (CSIRO). 2011. *Climate Change in the Pacific: Scientific Assessment and New Research. Volume 1: Regional Overview*.

Diamond, H.J., A.M. Lorrey, K.R. Knapp, and D.H. Levinson. 2012. Development of an enhanced tropical cyclone tracks database for the southwest Pacific from 1840–2011. *International Journal of Climatology*, 32: 2240–2250. DOI:10.1002/joc.2412.

International Monetary Fund (IMF). *IMF Country Report No.16/183*

Organisation for Economic Co-operation and Development (OECD). 2005. The Costs and Benefits of Trade Facilitation. *OECD Policy Brief*. October.

www.ingramcontent.com/pod-product-compliance
Lightning Source LLC
Chambersburg PA
CBHW060941170426
43195CB00026B/3000